Optimizing the Display and Interpretation of Data

Optimizing the Display
and Interpretation of Data

Robert A. Warner, MD

ELSEVIER

AMSTERDAM • BOSTON • HEIDELBERG • LONDON
NEW YORK • OXFORD • PARIS • SAN DIEGO
SAN FRANCISCO • SINGAPORE • SYDNEY • TOKYO

Elsevier
Radarweg 29, PO Box 211, 1000 AE Amsterdam, Netherlands
The Boulevard, Langford Lane, Kidlington, Oxford OX5 1GB, UK
225 Wyman Street, Waltham, MA 02451, USA

Notices
Knowledge and best practice in this field are constantly changing. As new research and experience
broaden our understanding, changes in research methods, professional practices, or medical treatment may become necessary.

Practitioners and researchers must always rely on their own experience and knowledge in evaluating
and using any information, methods, compounds, or experiments described herein. In using such
information or methods they should be mindful of their own safety and the safety of others, including parties for whom they have a professional responsibility.

To the fullest extent of the law, neither the Publisher nor the authors, contributors, or editors, assume
any liability for any injury and/or damage to persons or property as a matter of products liability,
negligence or otherwise, or from any use or operation of any methods, products, instructions, or
ideas contained in the material herein.

ISBN: 978-0-12-804513-8

British Library Cataloguing-in-Publication Data
A catalogue record for this book is available from the British Library

Library of Congress Cataloging-in-Publication Data
A catalog record for this book is available from the Library of Congress

For information on all Elsevier publications
visit our website at http://store.elsevier.com/

Working together
to grow libraries in
developing countries

www.elsevier.com • www.bookaid.org

Dedication

To Norma – my wife, my partner, my friend

CONTENTS

This book is intended for readers of many different backgrounds and interests. It is for those who wish to benefit as much as possible from the enormous quantities of computerized data that have become part of modern life. The book describes methods for displaying these data in ways that are especially meaningful and permit one to review even very large sets of data comprehensively and efficiently. The methods were developed to reveal all the useful information that the data had been collected to provide. The book also provides the scientific evidence that supports the use of each of the methods by demonstrating its accuracy and efficiency.

Each of these methods may be used with familiar commercial software that is already in widespread use. In fact, part of the description of the method includes the specific steps needed to use it with currently available programs, such as spreadsheet software. On the other hand, those skilled in developing computer hardware and software may also wish to adapt any of the described methods to devices and systems intended for general or specific commercial applications.

What was my personal reason for writing this book? My major reason for writing it concerns a long series of observations that I had made during my career as a hospital-based cardiologist. During that period, I had seen many examples of the need to have enough accurate information to provide good care for patients, but had been frustrated by the difficulties encountered in obtaining that information. To be sure, enormous amounts of electronically recorded and stored data are obtained in the course of providing nursing and medical care to both hospitalized and ambulatory patients. The development of increasingly sophisticated diagnostic instruments and improved methods of data storage have produced rapid increases in the amount and diversity of this information. To be useful, however, the information must be easily accessible to those who have the responsibility of providing their patients with the best possible care. Regardless of its intended benefit, information that has been collected but which cannot be accessed in a sufficiently timely fashion is useless.

To emphasize this, I will share with the reader an abbreviation that is often used by medical professionals in the context of diagnostic testing. "WNL" often appears in medical records and is supposed to stand for "within normal limits." This means that some diagnostic test produced a result that was within the range of values expected in a person who did not have the disease for which that test was relevant. All too often, though, "WNL" really stands for something quite different. It sometimes stands for "we never looked." In the instances when "WNL" has the latter meaning, it indicates that however beneficial to the patient's care the information provided by the test *might* have been, the patient's caregivers had remained unaware of it.

All too often, being unaware of important information can be attributed to serious obstacles encountered in accessing it. One of these obstacles is the sheer volume of computerized data being collected from patients. Although these data are usually stored for possible subsequent review by healthcare professionals, the time required for such review is often very great and would prevent these professionals from attending to their other important duties. For example, consider a patient who has been in an intensive care unit for 3 days. During this period, the values of five different clinical parameters were sequentially recorded and stored with each of the patient's heartbeats (average pulse rate of 80 beats/min). This example of the common practice of clinical monitoring would produce the following amount of data that must be reviewed:

$$5 \text{ parameters} \times 80 \text{ beats/min} \times 60 \text{ min/h} \times 24 \text{ h/day} \times 3 \text{ days}$$
$$= 1,728,000 \text{ data points}$$

As a gentle reminder, this is for only one patient! Hospital intensive care units, coronary care units, chest pain units, surgical care units, operating suites, and recovery rooms typically accommodate several patients at the same time.

It is also clear that this problem of "data overload" is by no means confined to the biomedical field. Individuals in many different fields often face the task of analyzing large quantities of digital and analog data in the pursuit of their occupational and personal interests. The efficient review and reliable interpretation of computerized data are critical for many fields including engineering, physical science, business management, and personal finance.

Furthermore, the growth of the Internet has made extremely large amounts of frequently updated computerized data available to serve the occupational, professional, and personal needs of millions. An important feature of the methods of data display, review and analysis that are described in this book is that they are "scalable." That is, each method can be adapted to sets of data from the very small to the very large.

The methods of displaying data were not chosen for aesthetic reasons. Instead, they and the various described techniques for interpreting the data were selected because the author's research has shown that they accurately and efficiently portray the useful information that the data contain. This is not to deny the importance of displaying data in attractive ways. Certainly, it is often important to present information at scientific, professional, and business meetings in visually pleasing ways. Similarly, commercial applications of any of the described methods of displaying data should be attractive to potential customers. Nevertheless, the purpose of this book is to help its readers attain knowledge about aspects of the world that are of greatest interest to them and are relevant to their goals and needs.

Properly used, our access to computerized data can provide us with unprecedented opportunities for professional and personal growth. Therefore, the methods described in this book are becoming increasingly relevant to life in the modern world. The book is intended to help its readers take advantage of those opportunities and benefit as much as possible from the vast treasure chest of information that contemporary technology can and should provide to them.

COMPANION WEBSITE

The images contained in this book are visible in full color at the book's companion site: booksite.elsevier.com/9780128045138.

AUTHOR BIOGRAPHY

Robert A. Warner, MD, is board-certified in both Internal Medicine and Cardiology and is currently living and working near Portland, OR. He received his BS degree from Union College in 1964 and his MD degree from Upstate Medical Center in 1969. He completed a residency in internal medicine at Upstate in 1972 and a fellowship in cardiology at Duke University Medical Center in 1975. He was an Eliphalet Nott Scholar at Union College and is a member of the Phi Beta Kappa, Sigma Xi and Alpha Omega Alpha honor societies. Dr Warner was a member of the faculty of Upstate Medical Center College of Medicine from 1975 to 1998 where he rose to the rank of Full Professor of Medicine. From 1986 to 1996, he served as Chief of the Medical Service at the Syracuse VA Medical Center. From 1998 to 2002, Dr Warner did medical research at the Duke University Clinical Research Institute in Durham, NC and from 2002 to 2006 served as the Medical Director of Inovise Medical, Inc. in Portland, OR. Since then, he has remained active in research, continues to publish in medical and computer science journals, and frequently presents his research findings at scientific meetings. Most of his current work consists of improving the accuracy of medical diagnoses and optimizing the interpretation of computer-generated data. The methods of interpretation that he has developed apply not only to biomedical data, but are also relevant to such diverse fields as engineering, the physical and social sciences, business, and personal finance. Dr Warner is the author of over 75 papers and 95 abstracts that have been published in peer-reviewed journals. He has served as consultant to many companies in the medical device and pharmaceutical industries and is the holder of four patents that are all related to the display and interpretation of biomedical data.

CHAPTER *1*

The Scope and Importance of Computerized Data

At the present time, computers generate enormous amounts of electronic data that are intended to serve the diverse needs of many people throughout the world. The availability of personal computers, in conjunction with access to the Internet, has helped many to use to these data to achieve their professional, commercial, and individual goals. Since computerized information can serve many important purposes, it is crucial that there be practical methods for using it most effectively. Features of such methods certainly include the need to interpret the data correctly. Also, the sheer volume of data available to us has also made it important that these methods enable us to review and analyze the data efficiently. Such reviews and analyses must be comprehensive. In other words, the speed with which one can review and analyze data should not come at the price of ignoring or discarding information that may be important.

Also, to be of greatest general use, our methods of displaying, reviewing, and analyzing data should be flexible and easy to employ. For example, a broadly applicable method that uses commonly available software is likely to be useful to more people than a method that requires the skills of computer programmers to accomplish only a highly specific task.

Optimal methods for displaying, reviewing, and interpreting computerized data can benefit people of many different interests and occupations. Such individuals include nurses, physicians, individual investors, businessmen, financial analysts, social scientists, engineers, economists, geologists, actuaries, political pollsters, and meteorologists.

The output of computers typically consists of digital data, i.e., numbers. Surely, there are plenty of different ways of analyzing numerical data. However, many of these methods, such as various types of mathematical modeling, generally require considerable training and skill in mathematics and statistics. In contrast, more intuitive ways of handling numerical data are available. For example, it is often advantageous to display the digital data not as numbers *per se*, but rather as pictorial images. We do this whenever we use the numbers to produce graphs of the data. In other words, we can often benefit from transforming the information provided by the computer from digital to analog form. For example, individual investors and investment professionals often employ "technical analysis" to try to predict whether the prices of stocks, bonds, mutual funds, and exchange-traded funds will rise or fall in the future. Technical analysis consists of studying previous patterns of variation in the prices of these securities. The investors and professional analysts hope that certain patterns of price fluctuation shown by these "technical charts" will help them buy securities when the prices are low and sell them when the prices are higher. Table 1.1 shows digital data that represent the closing prices in dollars of a security that mirrors the S&P 500 Index during the preceding 12-month period. Each number is the closing price in dollars of that security for each trading day of the previous year. The numbers are arranged in order from left to right and top to bottom, in the same fashion as the words on a page of English text. The information shown in Figure 1.1 is identical to that in Table 1.1, but is provided in analog, rather than in digital form. Figure 1.1 is simply a line graph of the digital data in Table 1.1 and shows, from left to right, the daily changes in the closing price of the security during the same 12-month period. Figure 1.1 is an example of a "technical chart." The column of numbers on the left side of the graph represents the security's closing price in dollars. Table 1.1 and Figure 1.1 contain identical information. However, the analog presentation of the information in Figure 1.1 makes it much easier to detect temporal patterns in the fluctuations of the security's price than is possible by examining the digital data in Table 1.1.

Seismography is another field that demonstrates the value of presenting data in analog form. Geologists rely on seismographs to record the tremors in the earth that are often associated with impending earthquakes or volcanoes. Modern seismographs are digital devices that record the changing amplitudes and frequencies of these tremors as sequential series of numbers. However, seismograms typically display the recorded data as line graphs that are based on those numbers. This is

Table 1.1 Digital Representation of a Security's Closing Prices in Dollars								
182.89	182.36	183.48	183.52	183.64	184.14	181.69	183.67	184.66
183.64	184.18	184.3	182.79	178.89	178.01	179.07	177.35	179.23
174.17	175.39	175.17	177.48	179.68	180.01	181.98	182.07	183.01
184.24	183.02	184.1	183.89	184.91	184.84	184.85	185.82	186.29
187.58	187.75	188.18	188.26	188.16	187.23	187.28	185.18	184.66
187.66	186.66	187.75	186.2	185.43	186.31	184.97	184.58	185.49
188.25	188.88	188.63	186.4	184.34	185.1	187.09	183.16	181.51
184.2	186.13	186.39	187.04	187.89	187.45	187.83	186.29	186.88
188.31	188.33	188.06	188.42	186.78	187.88	187.68	187.96	189.79
189.06	187.4	188.05	188.74	187.55	189.13	189.59	190.35	191.52
192.37	192.68	192.9	192.8	193.19	194.45	195.38	195.58	195.6
193.54	194.13	194.29	194.83	196.26	196.48	195.94	195.88	194.7
195.44	195.82	195.72	197.03	197.23	197.96	195.71	197.71	197.34
198.64	198.65	197.72	197.8	196.95	196.98	193.09	192.5	193.89
192.07	191.03	193.24	193.8	193.53	194.84	195.76	195.72	197.36
198.92	199.5	199.19	200.2	200.33	200.25	200.14	200.71	200.61
200.21	201.11	200.59	199.32	200.07	200.3	199.13	198.98	200.48
201.82	200.7	199.15	198.01	199.56	196.34	197.9	197.54	197.02
194.38	196.52	196.29	193.26	196.64	192.74	190.54	187.41	187.7
186.27	188.47	190.3	194.07	192.69	194.93	196.43	196.16	198.41
199.38	201.66	201.77	201.07	202.34	203.15	203.34	203.98	204.18
204.19	204.24	204.37	205.55	205.22	205.58	206.68	207.26	207.11
207.2	205.76	207.09	207.89	207.66	208	206.61	206.47	203.16
200.89	199.51	197.91	201.79	206.78	206.52	207.47	207.75	207.77
208.72	207.6	205.54	205.43	201.72	199.82	202.31	205.9	204.25
202.08								

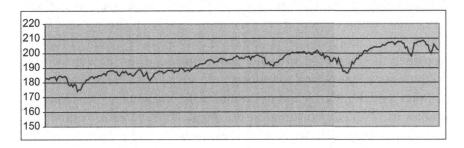

Fig. 1.1. Analog representation of the data in Table 1.1.

because it is easier to identify important patterns in the amplitudes and frequencies of seismographic data by examining the graphs than it is by reviewing the arrays of digits that were used to generate the graphs.

An even more common example of the conversion of data from a digital to an analog form is the electrocardiogram (ECG). This conversion greatly facilitates the identification of important diagnostic patterns in the ECG. An ECG machine is a galvanometer, a device that records voltages. In an ECG, the recorded voltages are those that are sequentially generated by heart tissue during the various phases of the cardiac cycle. It is certainly possible to obtain diagnostic information by examining the digital data that the ECG machine has recorded from a patient. However, to improve the identification of diagnostically important patterns in this information, the digital data are displayed in analog form. This analog representation of the changes in the heart's electrical activity over time is the familiar standard ECG recording. Facilitating the recognition of patterns in this way is especially important because the typical ECG recorded from a patient consists of 12 different sets of voltage data, corresponding to each of the 12 standard ECG "leads." Therefore, patterns of possible diagnostic importance for each patient must be detected not in only one set of data, but also in all 12 different sets of data. Furthermore, correct ECG interpretation also requires that these 12 different sets of data be compared with each other. It is much easier for an electrocardiographer to perform all these individual and comparative examinations and analyses of the data if the ECG information is represented in analog form, rather than as 12 large and separate aggregations of numbers.

It's not surprising that the generation of graphs from numerical data is highly useful. Humans are extremely skilled at recognizing patterns. For example, each of us may easily have seen thousands of different faces during our lives. However, we would probably instantly recognize the face of a previous acquaintance, even though we may not have seen that person for a long time. Our great ability to interpret complex visual patterns and discriminate among similar ones typically enables us to quickly distinguish our acquaintance's face from all the many other faces that we've seen previously. A major purpose of the various methods of data analysis described in this book is to allow us to take advantage of our inherent ability to detect meaningful patterns.

The importance of pattern recognition in the analysis of data is supported by a recent article on the front page of a major American newspaper. This article called attention to the problem of "Big Data overload" and to the necessity of being able to recognize patterns in scientific and in other types of data [1]. The approach described in the newspaper article is to provide "perceptual training" to enhance people's abilities to recognize patterns in data that they are examining.

However, while acknowledging that it is desirable to improve one's skills in a variety of ways, the present book offers a different approach. In this book, the author describes methods of presenting data in ways that make it easier and faster for people to detect meaningful patterns in the information. This approach permits us to take full advantage of the skills in pattern recognition that we already have. It will enable us to recognize and interpret important patterns in data, even by those with limited levels of training and skill in a particular field. It is not the author's intent to deny the value of expertise in people who review data. In numerous contexts, the eye will often fail to see what the brain does not know. For example, patterns in an ECG that are very meaningful to a cardiologist may well be unnoticed by a person in a different field. Similarly, the important features of a particular seismogram would likely be most apparent to a geologist who has been trained in seismographic interpretation.

It is entirely possible, however, to generate displays of data that are highly intuitive, regardless of the nature of the data to which they are applied. Such displays would reveal easily detectable patterns in the data that could then be interpreted in the appropriate context by individuals with the requisite background and skill.

Just as it is often advantageous to convert digital data to analog form, i.e., transform numbers into pictures, there are other circumstances in which it is valuable to do the reverse. This is because it may be useful to accurately quantify components of the patterns that the analog displays of the data have revealed. For example, a line graph of a set of numerical data may reveal possibly meaningful patterns of upward or downward deflections of the line. To characterize these identified patterns as accurately as possible, it is often useful to quantify the amplitudes and durations of these deviations. Visually examining the line graph itself can yield approximations of the magnitudes of the amplitudes and durations. However, the digital data from which the line graph was generated usually provide much more precise measurements of these amplitudes and durations than does visual inspection of the graph. The more precise measurements that are made possible by the digital data themselves can often be downloaded for storage and analysis. These precise digital measurements then constitute another set of data, e.g., to be used for developing especially accurate criteria for detecting events and phenomena of interest.

For each of the methods of the display, review, and analysis of data that are presented in this book, there is a description of the types of applications for which it is especially appropriate, as well as examples of these applications. None of the methods described in the book require special training or skill in mathematics, statistics, or computer science. For example, none of the methods involve processes such as complex mathematical modeling or advanced analytical techniques that not only require special expertise, but also often use highly specific computer programs to perform. Instead, each of the methods described in the book are easy to learn and can be implemented using the features contained in widely used personal computer programs. It is likely that many of the book's readers are already familiar with these programs. Therefore, this book describes how the computer hardware and software available to us can help us make the best use of the abundant sets of data that have become an integral part of the modern world.

It is also important to emphasize that the methods described in each chapter are not mutually exclusive. Instead, they can often be combined to produce especially powerful tools for maximizing the usefulness of the data available to us.

Regardless of our occupational needs, our professional interests, or our personal goals, we benefit others and ourselves by learning, as completely as possible, the truth about the world in which we live. It is therefore important for us to use, as effectively as possible, the rich sources of information that modern technology is making available to us. The author believes that this book will help its readers attain that goal. By so doing, it will help satisfy what the philosopher Immanuel Kant called, "our restless endeavor to make sense of things."

REFERENCE

[1] Learning to see data. New York Times. Available from: http://www.nytimes.com (accessed 29.03.2015).

CHAPTER 2

Using Z Scores for the Display and Analysis of Data

DESCRIPTION AND CALCULATION OF Z SCORES

A very frequent and important reason for reviewing sets of data is to identify outliers. Outliers are members of a dataset whose values seem to be higher or lower than the values of most of the other members of the dataset. If apparent outliers are detected, then it is necessary to ask, "Are any of them truly abnormal in some way, or are they unimportant because they are merely expected and inconsequential variations in the data?" For example, shortly before taking off on a scheduled flight, a pilot and copilot of a commercial airliner are reviewing an electronic display of measurements that are used to monitor the functioning of their plane's jet engines. They observe that for one of the engines, some of the values of the measurements of generated power appear to be lower than they had previously been. What should the flight crew conclude from these observations? Do the lower observed values represent expected fluctuations in the measured performance of a normally functioning jet engine, or do they represent important evidence that the engine is at significantly increased risk of failure? Should they proceed with the flight as scheduled, or should they cancel it?

This chapter will describe the use of Z scores (also called standard scores) as an effective tool for answering questions of this type. A Z score is the difference, expressed in standard deviations (SDs), between the value of a data point and the value of the mean of a population of data to which that data point is being compared. As will be shown, one can easily calculate a Z score for each member of a database. A major advantage of using Z scores rather than only the raw data is that each calculated Z score is associated with a P value. In statistics, P values are most commonly used for of comparing groups of data to one another. However, in the case of Z scores, the P values are used to compare the value of each member of a database to the average value of a population of data. The population of data whose average value is used for this comparison may be the same population to which each of the data points belongs. However, depending on the purpose of the comparison, it may be a different population of a similar type of data.

Regardless of the context in which it is used, a P value expresses the likelihood that an observed difference in the data is random, i.e., due only to chance. For instance, if the P value associated with the Z score of a particular data point is 0.05, it means that there is only a 5% chance that the observed difference between that data point and the mean of its comparison population is due merely to chance. If the P value associated with the Z score of another data point is 0.01, it means that the likelihood of such a difference being due merely to chance is only 1%. Thus, Z scores provide a statistically based estimate of how unusual it is for each individual value of a data point to be different from the mean of the population of data to which it is being compared [1].

Computers have made it extremely easy to perform the calculations needed to produce a Z score for each member of a database, even if that database is very large. To calculate a Z score, it is first necessary for the computer to calculate both the arithmetic mean (what is usually meant by "average") and the SD of the values of all the members of the comparison database. The mean of a population of data is a measure of central tendency of the data (as are the median and the mode). The arithmetic mean is calculated by dividing the sum of all the values of the data in the population by the number of data points in the same population. For example, if there are 14 individual data points in a population and their sum is 632, the mean = 632/14 = 45.14.

The SD is a measure of the amount of dispersion of the data, i.e., how much the individual values of all the members of the database tend to differ from one another. The larger the SD, the greater is the amount of variation among the individual data points in the population of data being analyzed. i.e., the more the values of individual data points tend to differ from each other and from the mean of the population to which they belong. The SD is given by the formula:

$$SD = sqrt\left[\frac{\Sigma(X_i - X)^2}{N}\right]$$

In this formula, sqrt = square root, Σ = sum, X_i = the value of an individual data point, X = the mean of the data population, and N = the number of different data points. Therefore, to calculate the SD, one follows these steps:

1. subtract the value of each data point from the mean of the population
2. square each of these differences. Please note that because the $(X_i - X)$ term in the formula is squared, the calculated SD is always positive, even if the value of X is greater than the value of X_i. This is important to remember for the interpretation of Z scores. Since the calculation of Z scores requires dividing by the SD, one always is dividing by a positive number. Therefore, the algebraic sign of a calculated Z score depends only on whether the individual value is greater or less than the population mean.
3. add up all the squared differences
4. divide the resulting sum of the squared differences by the number of data points in the population
5. obtain the square root of the result of this division

Figure 2.1 illustrates the principles behind the use of Z scores. Figure 2.1 shows the distribution of the individual values in a database. Figure 2.1 exemplifies a histogram of data – a line graph in which the horizontal axis of the graph shows the individual measured values of

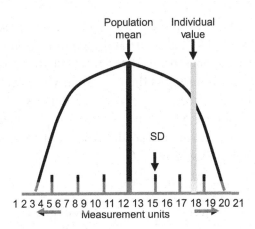

Fig. 2.1. Measuring variation in the data.

whatever parameter is appropriate for the data, and the vertical axis indicates the frequencies with each of these values occur. In Figure 2.1, the measurement values are shown below the X-axis in increasing order from left to right, and the most frequently observed values are between about 11.0 and 13.0.

Also, Figure 2.1 shows a series of much shorter black and gray lines above and perpendicular to the X-axis. The distance between each of the short black lines is one SD of that population of data. Since these shorter lines are 1.8 measurement units apart, the SD of this set of data is 1.8. Figure 2.1 shows that the measured values of the data have a normal, i.e., Gaussian, distribution. A normal distribution is a set of numerical values whose histogram is in the form of a bell-shaped curve. In Figure 2.1, the mean value of the data has a value of about 12.4 measurement units and is indicated by the tall, thick black vertical line in the center of the histogram. The tall, thick gray vertical line to the right of the population mean represents the value of a single data point from the same set of data and has a value of about 17.8 measurement units. Figure 2.1 shows that one way to express the difference between an individual data point and the population's mean is to use the relevant measurement units. Expressed algebraically, this difference is $17.8 - 12.4 = 5.4$ measurement units. The fact that the result of this sample calculation is a positive rather than a negative number means that the individual data point's value is numerically greater than the mean of the population to which the data point belongs.

Besides using the measurement units themselves to express the difference between an individual value and the population mean, one can also express this difference using the data population's calculated SD. As Figure 2.1 shows, not only is the individual value designated by the tall bluish-gray line 5.4 *measurement units* greater than the population's mean, it is also about 2.6 *SDs* above the population's mean. Therefore, in the example shown in Figure 2.1, the Z score of the individual value indicated by the tall gray line is +2.6.

The formula for calculating Z scores is:

$$Z \text{ score} = \frac{\text{Individual value} - \text{Population mean}}{\text{Population SD}}$$

If it were necessary to perform the above calculations (especially for the SD) by hand, it would be very tedious. Fortunately, however, many personal computer programs, such as spreadsheet software, have built-in functions that quickly calculate the means and SDs of numerical data. Therefore, when analyzing data using the personal computer, it is extremely easy to calculate Z scores for all the members of a database. The steps needed to calculate and use Z scores with a personal computer will be described later in this chapter.

ADVANTAGES OF Z SCORES FOR DISPLAYING AND ANALYZING DATA

However easy it is to calculate Z scores, why bother with them at all? Why not just use the original measurement units to express each numerical difference between an individual data point and the mean of the population of data to which the data point belongs? Z scores have several important properties that benefit the analysis of data. Z scores:

- *Indicate the Statistical Significance of Differences* – As noted above, in a set of normally distributed data, the absolute value of each Z score is associated with a *P* value (also called alpha). Table 2.1 shows three examples of the relationships between a given Z score and a *P* value.

  For example, if the calculated Z score of a data point = 1.85, Table 2.1 shows that its associated *P* value is between <0.05 and <0.01. This means that there is less than one chance in 20 and greater than one chance in 100 that this difference between the data point and the mean of the population can be attributed merely to chance. If the Z score of a data point = 2.62, it means that there is less than one chance in 100 and greater than one chance in 1,000

Table 2.1 Relationships Between Z Scores and *P* Values	
Z Score	*P* Value
≥ 1.65	<0.05
≥ 2.33	<0.01
≥ 3.08	<0.001

that the difference is due only to chance. If the Z score $=3.96$, it means that there is less than one chance in 1000 that the difference between the data point and the mean of the population is due only to chance. It is important to emphasize that the Z scores listed in Table 2.1 are the *absolute values* of the Z scores. In other words, there is the same relationship between a Z score and its corresponding P value, whether the data point is larger or smaller than the mean of the population to which the data point is being compared.

Z scores are broadly analogous to the well-known T test in statistics. Both Z scores and the T test are used to test the null hypothesis, i.e., to determine the likelihood that there is no meaningful difference from the mean of a comparison population. Whereas a Z score tests the null hypothesis concerning the difference between each data point and the mean of a comparison population, the T test tests the null hypothesis concerning the means of two different populations of data.

It is important to be able to test the null hypothesis for individual data points. This is because the individual values in most sets of data can be expected to vary to some extent. Using Z scores permits one to determine for each data point that differs from a population's mean, whether it is likely to represent a true abnormality or to merely be an example of the expected random variation among the values in a population of data.

One way to regard the Z score is as a tool for solving the classical problem of distinguishing between signal and noise. In the context of data analysis, noise consists of chance variations among the values of data points that fail to reveal meaningful information. In the present context, statistically significant Z scores indicate which members of a set of data are most likely to represent an actual signal, i.e., to convey meaningful information. Conversely, statistically insignificant Z scores are more to indicate data points that represent random noise. The determination of what P value should be considered to indicate a statistically significant difference depends upon various factors. One factor is whether it is considered more important not to miss a given abnormality (such as a very serious medical condition) or more important not to incorrectly identify apparent abnormalities whose presence would be inconsequential. Another factor is whether one is making comparisons that involve only one versus several different parameters. Comparisons involving multiple parameters require more stringent *P* values and therefore higher absolute values of Z scores. If the context in which the comparison of the data requires greater stringency, then lower *P* values and their correspondingly higher Z scores can be selected.

- *Show the Directions of the Differences Between the Mean and the Data Points of Interest* – It is important to emphasize again that the relationships between Z scores and *P* values illustrated in Table 2.1 refers to the absolute values of the Z score. As the formula for Z scores shows, a Z score can be either positive or negative, depending entirely on whether the measured value of the individual data point is larger or smaller than the calculated mean of the population. Therefore, if the algebraic sign of the Z score is positive, it means that individual data point is larger than the mean, and the reverse is true if the algebraic sign is negative. These are reliable conclusions because, as noted above, the SD by which the difference between the individual data point and the population mean is divided is always positive.

- *Express All Parameters on the Same Scale* – When reviewing data in either digital or analog form, it is often desirable to look for simultaneous changes in two or more different parameters. For example, in a medical unit, the doctors and nurses might wish to simultaneously display on the electronic monitors variations in blood pressure and oxygen saturation at the same time. Unfortunately, different parameters are often measured, using units that have widely different scales. This means that setting the scale of a display to show a parameter measured in numerically large units can drown out the display of parameters that are measured in smaller units. A solution to this problem is to display all the parameters using Z scores, rather than the raw data of the parameters in their original units of measurements. This is because Z scores display all parameters on the same scale – the SD [2]. Figure 2.2 illustrates the importance of this feature of Z scores. It shows line graphs of two different medical parameters being

simultaneously monitored in a hospital's intensive care unit.
Parameter A is measured in much larger numerical units than
Parameter B. The upper panel of Figure 2.2 shows line graphs of the
raw data of both parameters, i.e., both parameters displayed in their
original units of measurements. The temporal changes in the values
of Parameter A are easy to see. However, because of the smaller
scale of its units of measurements, it is very hard to see if there are
any changes in the recorded values of Parameter B. In contrast,
the lower panel displays the same information expressed in Z
scores, rather than in the original units of measurement. Since both
Parameters A and B are now displayed on the same scale (the SD),
it is now easy to compare the temporal changes in both parameters.
Figure 2.2 shows that displaying both parameters as their Z scores
provide another advantage. Since the units of both parameters are
now expressed in Z scores (which are displayed on the left vertical
axis of the graph), one can quickly see if any of their deviations
above or below the zero line of the graph are statistically significant.
In other words, are any of the observed changes in the values of
either parameter likely to be inconsequential, or are they likely to
be important? In the lower panel of Figure 2.2, any part of either

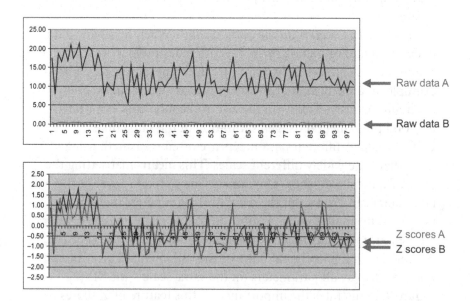

Fig. 2.2. Z scores and different scales of measurement.

line graph that exceeded a Z score of 1.65 or fell below a Z score of
−1.65 is significantly abnormal at a *P* value <0.05.

Besides permitting multiple parameters to be meaningfully displayed
on the same screen or page, expressing the various parameters
on the same scale confers an important perceptual advantage on
the reviewer of the data. If the various parameters being shown
are being expressed on different scales, it makes it difficult for
the reviewer to decide if a given change in one or more of the
parameters is large or small compared to the baseline values.
For example, a visible slight increase or decrease in a parameter
measured in smaller scale units may actually be greater compared
to the baseline than an apparently greater change of a parameter
expressed in larger scale units. In other words, using Z scores rather
than the raw data relieves the reviewer of the burden of continually
adjusting his or her perception of what constitutes a large or a small
change in the data being displayed.

- *Provide Consistency of Interpretation Throughout the Entire Range
  of Values* – The interpretation of a given value of a Z score is the
  same, regardless of whether it is in the middle or at the upper or
  lower end of the distribution of the data being analyzed. This
  consistency throughout the entire range of values of the data
  facilitates the interpretation of data that are represented as Z scores.
  The consistency associated with Z scores is in contrast to the use of
  percentiles to describe differences among data points. For example,
  the significance of a change of a parameter's Z score from 0.0 to 1.0
  is of the same magnitude as a change from 6.8 to 7.8. Conversely, in
  a population of data, the difference between the 50th and the 51st
  percentile is very small, but the difference between the 99th and the
  100th percentile is infinite [3].

- *Facilitate the Choice of the Stringency of Standards of Comparison* –
  As Table 2.1 shows, each value of a Z score is associated with a
  particular *P* value. This makes it very easy to answer the question of
  how much difference there should be between a data point and the
  rest of the population for the data point to be considered abnormal.
  For some purposes, it may be very important not to miss even minor
  abnormalities in a set of data. In that case, high sensitivity (the
  ability of a test to correctly indicate that a condition of interest is
  present) in identification is considered more important than high

specificity (the ability of a test to correctly indicate that a condition of interest is *not* present). In such a case, one might choose relatively low Z scores associated with *P* values around 0.05. For other purposes, it may be more important not to identify cases that that are only mildly abnormal, i.e., to emphasize high specificity over high sensitivity. Under these circumstances, one would choose relatively high Z scores with correspondingly lower associated *P* values.

- *Provide Efficiency, Objectivity, and Uniformity in the Interpretation of Data* – The accuracy of the interpretation of data partly depends on the expertise, background, possible biases, diligence, and alertness of the persons who have the task of reviewing the information. For example, incorrect interpretation of data can result not only from inadequate expertise, but also from distraction or fatigue associated with the tedium of reviewing large amounts of information. However, using Z scores permits a more objective and consistent review of data that helps to overcome these limitations. This is because all Z scores are calculated using the same mathematical formula, and the interpretation of their associated *P* values conforms to well-established statistical principles. The resulting uniformity of interpretation, as well as the demonstrable soundness of conclusions based on the use of Z scores improves the reliability of the data analysis. As will be shown below, it is easy to produce displays of Z scores that permit the review of large amounts of data both accurately and efficiently. This helps relieve the tedium and fatigue often associated with the review of large collections of data.
- *Permit a Choice of Multiple Standards of Comparison* – As discussed, Z scores are calculated using the mean and SD that have been calculated for a particular set of data. An additional advantage of Z scores is that there are several different possible choices for the set of data used to calculate this mean and SD:
  - *Comparison of the Data Points to the Mean of the Same Set of Data* – In this case, the Z scores of each data point in a set of data are calculated using the mean and SD of the same set of data to which the data points belong. For example, the admissions committee of a university may want to choose from their pool of applicants the ones whose scores on a standardized college admissions test are significantly better than those of the others in the same group of applicants. The committee would

then calculate the Z score of each applicant's test score, using the mean and SD of the test scores of the same group to which the applicant belongs.

- *Comparison to a Known Normal Standard* – One can also calculate a Z score for each member of a data set whose normal versus abnormal status is unknown by using the mean and SD of a separate set of data that has been established by independent criteria to be normal. Any statistically significant Z score that is calculated in this way is significantly different from an established normal standard, rather than from the mean of the set of data from which the data point came. For example, a medical laboratory may have collected test data from a group of patients who are known by independent criteria not to have particular diseases. It then uses the mean and SD from that group of nondiseased patients to calculate Z scores for the patients whose status with respect to that disease is unknown. Each patient whose Z score for this parameter is both directionally appropriate and statistically significant when calculated in this way can be said to meet this diagnostic criterion for the disease [2,3].

- *Comparison to a Baseline Condition* – When collecting data over a given period, one can use the mean and SD of data that have been recorded during a baseline or resting period. This is often an important application of Z scores, especially when there are expected differences among the baseline conditions of individuals. This is because one is often interested not in any individual differences among different patients at the baseline, but instead what changes in the same patient are induced by a specific event or intervention. For example, in performing exercise testing for heart disease, one typically looks for measurable changes in the electrocardiogram (ECG) that are specifically associated with a particular type of exercise. Therefore, one can record the ECG data from a patient before the period of exercise begins. One then records the same type of ECG data while that patient is exercising and then calculates the Z scores for the exercise ECG data using the means and SDs of the pre-exercise data. Any statistically significant Z scores calculated in this way would represent exercise-induced abnormalities in that particular patient and are therefore likely to be diagnostically important.

The same principle often applies to monitoring patients in a hospital setting. The question is often not how a particular patient's recorded data compare to those of other patients, but how do those data change in the same patient when a particular event (such as an episode of chest pain or shortness of breath) occurs. This phenomenon is illustrated by Figure 2.4, which shows statistically significant changes from the resting condition in the values of five different parameters that occurred with the onset of an acute myocardial infarction (MI).

Using Z scores to evaluate changes in various parameters compared to a baseline condition is also relevant in studying the effects of deliberate interventions. For example, researchers could use Z scores to determine if the use of a particular drug (or dose of that drug) or other type of therapy produces statistically significant changes in relevant data recorded from an individual. An anesthesiologist could use the Z score method to monitor changes in certain physiological parameters to determine if the amount of anesthetic being given during an operation is likely to be adequate to protect the patient from experiencing pain while the surgery is being performed.

Comparing changes from a baseline condition using Z scores is by no means confined to biomedical applications. Quality control engineers may use the Z scores of appropriate data to detect evidence of impending failure of a mechanical or electrical device. Administrators may use Z scores of relevant parameters to determine if changes in various policies have had desirable or undesirable effects on the operations of a business. Police commanders may use Z scores of the crime rates of various precincts, streets, or neighborhoods to more appropriately guide the allocation of law enforcement resources. Because of the substantial loss of life and property often associated with seismic events, geologists may consider Z scores to evaluate changes in seismological data to help them predict the occurrence of earthquakes in an accurate and timely fashion. The possible use of Z scores in seismology will be discussed in much more detail later in this chapter.

In thinking about these and other possible applications for color-coded Z scores, it is interesting to note that there is already an established application for measuring differences among data using SDs. This is in the "six sigma" method that is widely used for monitoring quality control processes [4]. In statistics, the Greek letter sigma is the symbol for the SD.

DISPLAYING DATA USING Z SCORES

To interpret data both accurately and efficiently, it is important to optimize the ways in which the data are displayed. The properties of Z scores make it especially easy to present information in meaningful ways that quickly reveal important patterns in the data. The following are strategies for displaying and interpreting data using Z scores.

Color-Coding Z Scores to Identify Abnormalities

Table 2.2 shows a method for using various colors to identify data that have statistically significant Z scores. The first column of the table shows Z scores whose absolute values demarcate ranges of *P* values from 0.05 to 0.001. The second column of Table 2.2 suggests how Z scores can be color-coded to show the directions and magnitudes of statistically significant Z scores. On a color screen or printout, positive Z scores could be colored yellow, orange and red as their associated *P* values go from 0.05 to 0.01 to 0.001, respectively. Negative Z scores could go from light blue to dark blue to violet as their associated *P* values go from 0.05 to 0.01 to 0.001, respectively.

The third column demonstrates a method of displaying statistically significant Z scores if the devices that are being used to show the data can't display or print in full color. In the absence of full color, a gray scale is used to indicate data points that are significantly different from the mean to which they're being compared.

Table 2.2 Z Scores, *P* Values, and Color Coding		
Z Score	**Full Color P**	**Gray Scale P**
≥3.08	0.001	0.001
≥2.33	0.01	0.01
≥1.65	0.05	0.05
−1.64 to +1.64	NS	NS
≤−1.65	0.05	0.05
≤−2.33	0.01	0.01
≤−3.08	0.001	0.001

The color-coding of Z scores can be used for both analog and digital displays of data. Figures 2.3 and 2.4 suggest how color-coded Z scores can be applied to the field of electrocardiography. The ECG is a very commonly performed diagnostic test and its interpretation is a complex task that requires a considerable amount of training and experience to perform accurately. First, the signals recorded by each lead of the ECG have multiple parts that reflect the various phases of electrical depolarization and repolarization that take place in different regions of the heart during all the portions of the cardiac cycle. Second, the diagnostically important portions of the signal consist of numerous possible combinations of deflections from the ECG's baseline. Third, the standard ECG uses multiple leads that record the above information from the unique perspectives of 12 different positions on the body. Because of these positional differences, the values of the recorded measurements needed for diagnosis differ among all 12 leads. One of the first tasks in interpreting the ECG is for the electrocardiographer to determine whether any of the numerous possible deflections of a given ECG are abnormal in amplitude and/or duration. As expected, because of the many permutations of amplitude and duration that are possible among all the leads and portions of the ECG, it requires considerable time and experience to acquire that knowledge. However, Figure 2.3 suggests how color-coded Z scores can be used to quickly identify abnormalities of both amplitude and duration on the analog ECG display. Using the system of color-coding suggested for Table 2.2, portions of the ECG tracing can be colored

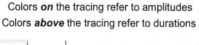

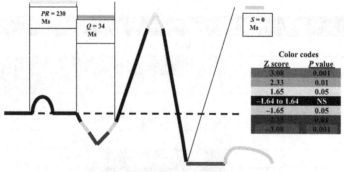

Fig. 2.3. Using color-coded Z scores to identify abnormalities on the analog ECG display.

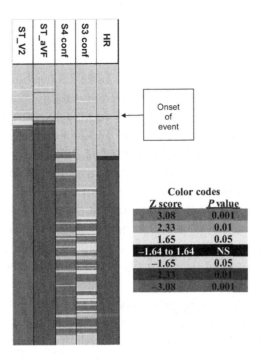

Fig. 2.4. Using Z scores to show significant changes in data over time. ST_V2, ST segment displacement in ECG lead V2; ST_aVF, ST segment displacement in ECG lead aVF; S4 Conf, fourth heart sound energy; S3 Conf, third heart sound energy; HR, heart rate.

if those portions have amplitudes or durations significantly greater or lesser, respectively, than those that would be expected in a normal ECG. The judgments of normal versus abnormal in each part of this analog display were made from the values of Z scores that were calculated using the means and SDs of the corresponding ECG measurements from a group of subjects known by independent criteria to be normal [5].

Precise measurements of both the amplitudes and durations of these deflections constitute the data used to diagnose various types of heart disease.

It is also important to note that a modern ECG machine acquires the data in digital form and subsequently generates the familiar analog ECG display using the graphing module that is part of the device's software. Therefore, an alternative to the traditional method of examining analog ECG waveforms is the analysis of the digital data that had been used to generate those waveforms. These digital data can be downloaded from the ECG machine to a personal computer, tablet, medical monitor, or similar device [5,6]. Table 2.3 suggests how color-coded Z scores can be used to facilitate the display and analysis of the digital ECG data that have been recorded from a patient. In Table 2.3, each column contains the measured values of the amplitudes and durations of eight different ECG parameters. The rows in Table 2.3 show the measurements that were obtained from each of the 12 standard ECG leads. Thus, the diagnostic matrix illustrated by Table 2.3 consists of 96 different values for this patient. The # symbol in each data-containing cell of the matrix would be the measured value of the parameter in a particular lead. These measured values are obtained from the stored data in the ECG machine and their units are microvolts for the amplitudes and milliseconds (ms) for the durations. On a color screen or printout, if the data point in a cell of the matrix has a Z score that is statistically significantly greater than the mean of the corresponding measurement in a group of normal subjects, the cell is colored either yellow, orange, or red. If the data point is significantly lower than the mean of the corresponding measurement in the normal database, then it is colored either light blue, dark blue or violet.

Just as an ECG machine produces an analog display using the voltage data that it has acquired from the patient, it could also generate such a matrix to accompany the standard analog ECG. By identifying

Table 2.3 Color-Coded Matrix of ECG Measurements								
Lead	Q Amp	Q Dur	R Amp	R Dur	S Amp	S Dur	ST Amp	T Amp
I	#	#	#	#	#	#	#	#
II	#	#	#	#	#	#	#	#
III	#	#	#	#	#	#	#	#
aVR	#	#	#	#	#	#	#	#
aVL	#	#	#	#	#	#	#	#
aVF	#	#	#	#	#	#	#	#
V1	#	#	#	#	#	#	#	#
V2	#	#	#	#	#	#	#	#
V3	#	#	#	#	#	#	#	#
V4	#	#	#	#	#	#	#	#
V5	#	#	#	#	#	#	#	#
V6	#	#	#	#	#	#	#	#
Amp, amplitude; dur, duration; Q, Q wave; R, R wave; S, S wave.								

statistically significant abnormalities in each ECG, the color-coded matrix would be a useful tool for improving the accuracy of ECG interpretation and for improving the skills of electrocardiographers. For example, in interpreting the standard analog ECG associated with the data in Table 2.3, an electrocardiographer might suspect that there are abnormally large Q waves in lead aVF. Looking at color-coded data of a type suggested by Table 2.3 would quickly confirm that both the amplitude and the duration of the Q waves (Q amp and Q dur) in lead aVF are statistically significantly greater than normal. This would be shown by the presence of yellow and the orange colors in the cells of the matrix at the intersections of row six and the first two columns of data. Color-coded matrices such as the one suggested in Table 2.3 could accompany each standard analog ECG so that the reader could compare his or her visual interpretation with the objective information provided by the colored-coded Z scores of each diagnostically important computerized measurement.

The interpretation of the ECG is further complicated by the fact that it is known that the normal ranges of values of amplitude and duration of ECG parameters vary with respect to the age and sex of the patient. It is also true that the age and sex of the patient are entered in the ECG machine's computer memory each time an ECG is recorded. Therefore, the normal databases used for calculating the color-coded Z score matrix could easily be age and sex-specific. The ability to select demographically appropriate sets of data for the calculation of the Z scores would further increase the accuracy of ECG interpretation that is based on Z scores.

Using Z Scores to Detect Changes in Data Over Time
It is often important to analyze time series of data to determine if there are quantitative changes in the data during a particular period. Examples of such circumstances include:

- engineers collecting data to assess the stability of the performance of an electrical or mechanical device during a particular period
- manufacturers monitoring the ongoing effectiveness of quality control initiatives
- meteorologists recording hourly changes in temperature and barometric pressure to help forecast the weather

- doctors and nurses trying to detect sequential changes in medical parameters that indicate changes in the clinical condition of a patient
- geologists recording seismic data over prolonged periods to seek evidence for possible impending earthquakes
- financial analysts following changes in various economic parameters over different periods to choose the nature and timing of investments
- political scientists studying demographic and economic trends

For these and similar tasks, how can we help ensure that we have not failed to detect any changes in the data that may have occurred and determined reliably whether any of them are significant or trivial? The use of color-coded Z scores addresses both of these questions.

A color screen or printout of Figure 2.4 shows a directionally appropriate Z score display of the changes in 5 different medical parameters over a period of about 20 min. These parameters were being continuously measured while the patient was undergoing a cardiac catheterization. In the course of the procedure, one of the patient's coronary arteries was inadvertently damaged so that blood flow through the artery was interrupted. As a result of this interruption, the patient sustained an acute MI (heart attack) and fortunately survived. Because of the circumstances under which the event occurred, the exact time and cardiac location of the MI is known. In Figure 2.4, the Z score display of the following five parameters is shown:

1. ST_V2 – a measurement in millimeters of the displacement (up or down) of the ST segment – part of the ECG – in standard ECG lead V2
2. ST_aVF – a measurement in millimeters of the displacement (up or down) of the ST segment – part of the ECG – in standard ECG lead aVF
3. S4 Conf – a measurement of the acoustical energy of the electronically recorded fourth heart sound – a sound commonly detected late in the diastolic (filling) portion of the cardiac cycle. Increased S4 intensity is a very common finding in acute MI [7].
4. S3 Conf – a measurement of the acoustical energy of the electronically recorded third heart sound – a sound commonly detected early in the diastolic portion of the cardiac cycle [8].

5. HR – the heart rate measured in beats per minute. Depending on the individual clinical circumstances, the heart rate may either increase of decrease as the result of an MI.

On a colored screen or printout, the Z score display shown in Figure 2.4 would show that the patient's MI was associated with statistically significant and directionally appropriate changes in all five of the above parameters. Specifically, a colored display would show that soon after the onset of the infarction, the ST segments of the patient's ECG increased in amplitude in lead V2 and simultaneously decreased in amplitude in lead aVF. Next, the fourth heart sound energy increased, and this was later followed by an increase in the third heart sound energy. In addition, the last column of Figure 2.4 would show in a color display that the patient's heart rate decreased.

The timing, nature, and direction of all the abnormalities shown in Figure 2.4 are completely consistent with an acute MI of a specific portion (the anterior wall) of the patient's left ventricle.

Figure 2.4 provides a real-life illustration of the most important properties of color-coded Z scores:

1. *Statistical Significance* – The striking changes in the display after the onset of the event show that the changes that occurred in all five of the diagnostic parameters were statistically significant and not merely a consequence of expected variations in the clinical data collected from a normal patient.
2. *Directions of the Changes* – A colored display would show whether the values of each of the parameters increased or decreased. Specifically, the recorded values ST_V2, S4 Conf, and S3 Conf increased significantly. Conversely, the recorded values ST aVF and HR decreased significantly. The respective directions of the changes in each of these parameters are exactly what would be expected in an acute MI.
3. *Display of the Parameters on the Same Scale* – Since Z scores express all parameters in the same units (the SD), observed quantitative changes in each of the parameters can be easily compared with each other. For example, the maximum value of S4 Conf and S3 Conf is 10 units. However, the maximum value of HR exceeds 300 beats/min. Therefore, using their original units, it would have been impossible to show simultaneous changes in all these parameters in a meaningful way.

The ability to show simultaneous statistically significant directional changes in multiple parameters is extremely important. In the case of Figure 2.4, this particular combination of the observed changes in each of the five displayed parameters represents very powerful evidence that the patient has sustained an acute MI. This is because the diagnosis is more likely to be correct if it is supported by appropriate changes in multiple parameters than if there had been only one type of evidence to support it. This type of confirmation is especially powerful if the parameters being used are generally orthogonal, i.e., causally independent of each other. Diagnoses supported by more redundant types of evidence are less certain. For example, in Figure 2.4, ST_V2 and ST_aVF are both ECG measurements and are therefore relatively redundant. However, the remaining three parameters are independent of the ECG and therefore provide strong support of the diagnosis suggested by the ECG.

4. *Choice of a Comparison Set of Data* – In the example shown in Figure 2.4, the most important question was whether or not there were significant changes in the patient's own physiological data following the onset of a specific event. In this case, the event was the inadvertent damage to the artery by the catheter. In the great majority of other cases that one is likely to encounter, the event associated with the observed changes in diagnostic parameters could be the onset of chest pain. Changes in appropriate parameters as illustrated in the color-coded Z scores in Figure 2.4 would strongly suggest that the chest pain was due to an MI rather than to a noncardiac cause. That is why the Z scores for each of the five parameters was calculated using the means and SDs of the data that had been collected from the same patient before the event had occurred. In other words, the patient served as her own control. For a different purpose, the Z scores could have been calculated using the means and SDs of data acquired from a separate population of patients. Once again, the use of Z scores permits one to choose the most appropriate reference population of data for the task at hand.

COLOR-CODED Z SCORES FOR DISPLAYING VERY LARGE AMOUNTS OF DATA

It is often necessary to review very large accumulations of data. Such datasets may represent information that has been collected previously, or they may consist of data that are still being recorded and examined in real time. Examples of the latter include the continuous monitoring of multiple medical parameters in coronary care units, intensive care units, emergency departments, operating rooms, and recovery rooms. The review of very large amounts of data can be expensive, especially if the review requires one or more highly skilled persons to complete it. Also, because of the tedium associated with the task, important abnormalities can be missed. An example of such a circumstance is ambulatory monitoring to detect abnormal heartbeats. Frequently, patients with known or suspected heart disease are asked to wear a portable device that records ECG information. These devices are typically worn from one to several days and may record and store data obtained simultaneously by several different ECG leads. The recorded ECG data are then downloaded to a stationary device and reviewed for any abnormalities that may have occurred during the period of recording. Many such ambulatory recordings are performed for both clinical purposes and for research. In either case, a recording from a given patient typically produces a very large amount of data for subsequent review. For example, in the case of a patient with a normal heart rate of 70 beats/min who is using a two-lead recording device to obtain a recording over a period of 3 days, there would be the following number of recorded heartbeats to examine:

$$70 \text{ beats/min} \times 60 \text{ min / h} \times 24 \text{ h / day} \times 3 \text{ days} \times 2 \text{ leads} = 604,800 \text{ beats}$$

Furthermore, even diagnostically important abnormalities of the ECG waveform (such as ST segment displacement of only 1 or 2 mm) can be very subtle and therefore can easily be missed because of the sheer volume of the ECG complexes that must be reviewed.

Computer algorithms have been devised to detect ECG abnormalities. However, as will be demonstrated later in this chapter, such algorithms often produce inaccurate diagnoses. Therefore, the review ECG data by skilled human interpreters is often preferred [9].

Figure 2.5 suggests how the use of color-coded Z scores can make possible rapid identification of all the significant abnormalities in very large sets of data. This can eliminate the need for the screening of the data by individuals with less expertise. Color-coded Z scores can therefore provide highly efficient full disclosure of all the possible abnormalities to the professionals who are responsible for providing the most accurate interpretations of the findings.

24-h display (March 4–March 5, 2014)

10 am	11 am	12 am	1 pm	2 pm	3 pm	4 pm	5 pm	6 pm	7 pm	8 pm	9 pm

10 pm	11 pm	12 pm	1 am	2 am	3 am	4 am	5 am	6 am	7 am	8 am	9 am

1-h display

6 pm	6:05 pm	6:10 pm	6:15 pm	6:20 pm	6:25 pm	

6:30 pm	6:35 pm	6:40 pm	6:45 pm	6:50 pm	6:55 pm	7:00 pm

Fig. 2.5. Color-coded Z scores for the rapid review of data (ST segment deviation).

Also regarding the question of expertise color-coded Z scores can reduce the need for highly trained specialists to identify abnormalities in large amounts of data that are being actively accumulated or have already been collected for various purposes. All that is needed for an observer to know that any abnormalities are present is for that person to see changes in the color of one or more parts of the display of data. No further expertise is required to make these initial observations. Once the abnormalities have been identified in this way, the expertise of the specialists can then be used to interpret their meaning and significance.

Figure 2.5 shows at two different time scales, how a color-coded Z score display of data can represent the amount of displacement of a patient's ST segments recorded during a 24-h period. The ST segment is a portion of the ECG signal whose periodic abnormal displacement either up or down often signifies that a patient is at increased risk for an MI or sudden death. Such periods of displacement of the ST segment typically last for at least several minutes. In each panel of Figure 2.5, the absence of color in the cells immediately above the listed times would indicate that there was no significant ST segment displacement during that period. Conversely, the presence of color indicates that there was statistically significant ST displacement during the period. In the upper panel, each rectangle represents 1 h and shows there was significant segment displacement between 6:00 pm and 7:00 pm, between 1:00 am and 2:00 am, and between 5:00 am and 6:00 am. The appearance of the colors blue or violet in any cell of the matrix would mean that the measurements of the ST segment had become more negative, i.e., displaced downward rather than upward. In the upper panel, the most severe displacement, as indicated by a violet color, occurred between 6:00 pm and 7:00 pm. The lower panel shows the 6:00 pm to 7:00 pm time period in greater detail because it represents a smaller time scale. Specifically, each rectangle in the lower panel now represents only 2.5 min rather than the 1-h period of the upper panel. A color display of the lower panel of Figure 2.5 would reveal that at slightly after 6:07 pm, the ST segment displacement begins, gradually increases in severity, remains most severe between 6:20 pm and about 6:27 pm and then gradually subsides until it has resolved at about 6:37 pm.

Figure 2.5 shows how matrices of color-coded Z scores can be used to interpret very large amounts of data both accurately and efficiently. An important part of the method consists of displaying the data at progressively smaller time scales. If any colors appear in the display that represent a larger time scale (e.g., the upper panel of Figure 2.5), it would immediately flag the fact that at least one significant abnormality has occurred during one relatively long interval of time. To obtain more details about any abnormality identified on the large time scale display, one would then "drill down" to a smaller time scale display (e.g., the lower panel of Figure 2.5). The more detailed information about the magnitudes and the time course of the ST segment displacement provided in lower panel is of great diagnostic importance. The type of ST segment displacement that characterizes serious heart disease persists for at least several minutes begins, gradually worsens, reaches its greatest degree of severity, and then gradually resolves. This is precisely the pattern that would be exhibited by color-coded Z score data in the lower panel of Figure 2.5.

The example shown in both panels of Figure 2.5 is particularly useful for demonstrating the advantages of color-coded Z scores. This is because compared to the ECG recording as a whole; ST segment displacement of only a very small amount is often associated with potentially life-threatening cardiac conditions (such as a heart attack or impending arrhythmias). For example, the amount of ST segment displacement associated with potentially lethal conditions is often only 1 or 2 mm.

In contrast, the total amplitude of the entire ECG complex may be greater than 40 mm. In other words, especially when reviewing a long recording, it is very easy to miss clinically important ST segment abnormalities because of their much smaller relative magnitudes. However, as the pair of diagnostic matrices in Figure 2.5 show, the color-coded Z score changes are very easy for a reviewer to see and then evaluate further.

Statistical Considerations

- Selection of P values – Z scores associated with P values of 0.05, 0.01, and 0.001 are shown in Tables 2.1 and 2.2 and Figures 2.3 and 2.4. P values of this magnitude are commonly used in research in the biomedical and social sciences. However, depending on the nature of the data and the specific purpose of the analysis, one may choose P values other than these to reject the null hypothesis. To incorrectly reject the null hypothesis, i.e., to conclude that a statistically significant difference exists when it really doesn't, is to commit a "Type 1" statistical error. For example, Type 1 errors can occur when statistical comparisons of more than two parameters are being made. To avoid committing Type 1 errors in a particular set of circumstances, one can choose more stringent P values. As Table 2.4 illustrates, there is a Z score associated with any P value that is desired.

Needless to say, color-coding can be applied to any set of Z scores that is deemed appropriate for the purpose at hand. In scientific studies, it is strongly recommended that the P value be chosen a priori, i.e., before the data are analyzed.

- Distribution of the Data – using Z scores to analyze data is the most appropriate when the data have Gaussian, i.e., normal distributions. This is analogous to the situation with the use of either paired or unpaired T tests to compare two populations of data. These

Table 2.4 Examples of Higher Z Scores Associated with More Stringent P Values	
Z Score	P Value
3.72	0.0001
4.26	0.00001
4.75	0.000001

"parametric" (the parameters being the means and SDs of the data) tests are appropriate if both of the populations are Gaussian. If histograms of the data show that their distributions are non-Gaussian, e.g., heavily skewed to the right or left, a less robust nonparametric test such as the Mann–Whitney U test should be substituted for the T test.

However, non-Gaussian data can often be transformed to normally distributed data by using the logarithms or the square roots of the raw data. Commonly used personal computer programs, such as spread-sheet software, have modules that can easily perform these mathematical transformations.

EVIDENCE SUPPORTING THE USEFULNESS OF Z SCORES

The advantages of using Z scores for analyzing data have been documented in several scientific studies [2,3,5]. For example, in a study of 1138 patients whose diagnoses were confirmed by cardiac catheterization, the use of Z scores had excellent sensitivity and specificity for diagnosing two different types of heart attacks – prior inferior MI and prior anterior MI. In fact, the performances of the Z score method were significantly superior to each of the two most widely used commercial computerized ECG diagnostic algorithms. The diagnostic performances of the Z score method were compared to the diagnostic performances of the commercial algorithms using the chi-square analysis. For inferior MI, comparing the superior Z score method to each of the algorithms yielded chi square = 43.9 ($P < 0.0000001$) and chi square = 20.3 ($P < 0.000001$), respectively. For anterior MI, comparing the superior Z score method to each of the algorithms yielded chi square = 24.1 ($P < 0.000001$) and chi square = 9.2 ($P < 0.002$), respectively [3]. The Z score method consists simply of determining whether the measurements of one or more diagnostically relevant ECG parameters are significantly different from the mean values of similar measurements in a population of patients known to have normal hearts by cardiac catheterization. Since all that is needed to make the correct diagnosis is to observe whether the relevant parameter of a given patient is colored in the display, a large number of ECG records can be reviewed in a short time. This is illustrated in Figure 2.7.

Also, Figure 2.4 shows the usefulness of color-coded Z scores for revealing significant abnormalities as they are occurring in an ongoing time series of data. As previously noted, Figure 2.4 demonstrates that color-coded Z scores are able to reveal the directions and magnitudes of the changes in the values of relevant diagnostic data that began immediately after the onset of an acute MI.

CALCULATING AND DISPLAYING Z SCORES ON A PERSONAL COMPUTER

Z scores can be very easily calculated and displayed using widely available commercial software, such as spreadsheet programs. This facilitates the use of Z scores for many different purposes. The following example illustrates the conversion of raw data to color-coded Z scores in a spreadsheet. In this example, the data shown in Table 2.5 are being compared to a database containing only values that by independent criteria are known to be normal. The values of the data in the normal database have a mean of 128.6 and a SD of 104.8. The left column of Table 2.5 shows 26 different data points that represent some of the measured values of the parameter being analyzed.

The Z scores shown in the right column of Table 2.5 are obtained for each row by subtracting 128.6 from the raw data value in that row and then dividing the difference by 104.8. One simply enters the formula (raw data value − 128.6)/104.8 in the first row of the Z score column and then copies that formula to the remaining rows in the same column.

In Microsoft Excel®, one can color the significant Z scores using the following steps:

- Highlight the column containing the calculated Z scores.
- Left click "Format" at the top of the screen.
- Left click "Conditional Formatting" in the pop-up window.
- In this pop-up window, select a range of values that you want to color. For example, if you want to color yellow each cell whose value is between 1.66 and 2.32, insert those numbers, respectively, in the boxes on each side of the word "and."
- After entering those numbers, left click "Format."
- In the window that pops up, left click "Patterns."

Table 2.5 Raw Data and Color-Coded Z Scores	
Raw Data	Z Score
66	−0.597
−24.9	−1.465
−95.3	−2.136
−93.5	−2.119
79.2	−0.471
188.5	0.572
−43.1	−1.638
−199.6	−3.132
−34.1	−1.552
384.6	2.443
71.9	−0.541
−59.3	−1.793
−8.6	−1.309
−213.5	−3.264
90.4	−0.365
−127	−2.439
−159.9	−2.753
168.5	0.381
−223.7	−3.362
−30.3	−1.516
−180.7	−2.951
−40.1	−1.610
−42.1	−1.629
−211.6	−3.246
−137.8	−2.542
−15.7	−1.377

- Left click the yellow cell from the palette of colors that appears, and then left click "Add."

For other significant values of Z scores, in the next window that pops up, select a different range of values and a different color for that range.

Unfortunately, a limitation of using the conditional formatting option to color-code the cells of a spreadsheet is that conditional formatting permits the simultaneous use of no more than three different colors.

To enable the use of more than three colors for coding a spreadsheet's cells, one can use the spreadsheet "sort" function. For example, one can sort the column containing the Z scores in ascending order. To do this, one can place the cursor in the first row of the column to be sorted and then left click the "A above Z" tab in the standard toolbar at the top left of the page. Alternatively, one can left click the "Data" tab at the top left of the page and then select the column to be sorted and whether the sort should be ascending or descending. When the Z scores are sorted in either ascending or descending order, it will be very easy to identify the cells that have Z score values that should be colored. This is because the sorting process brings together all the data in all the ranges of values that are of interest. One can then manually color the appropriate cells in those ranges using the "Fill Color" tab at the top right of the page. If desired, the rows of the spreadsheet can then be resorted to their original order.

A spreadsheet program can also be used to display efficiently very large amounts of colored Z score data. A way to do this is to compress the heights of the rows of a spreadsheet that contain such data. In Excel spreadsheets, the default height of a row is 12.75. To show this, right click any of the row numbers at the left side of the screen, then left click "Row Height," and the number 12.75 appears. The units that express row height in the spreadsheet are 1/72 in. Therefore, the default row height in Excel is $12.75 \times 1/72 = 0.18$ in. It follows that to display 100 rows of data at the default row height of 12.75 units requires 18 in. of vertical space. In contrast to this, Figure 2.6 suggests how a color-coded Z score display can be generated in Excel by both color-coding the cells based

Fig. 2.6. Compressed colored Z score display.

on the values of their Z scores and then compressing the heights of the spreadsheet's rows. The display in Figure 2.6 shows 100 rows of Z score data in a compressed format that obviously occupies far less vertical space than the 18-in. uncompressed display would have required.

Figure 2.7 shows how a compressed display of encoded Z scores can permit one to quickly identify diagnostically important patterns in a collection of data that was assembled to make diagnoses in each of a large number of patients. Figure 2.7 shows an encoded Z score display of the values of the measurements of an ECG parameter that is known to be abnormally large in patients with inferior MI – a common type of heart attack. This parameter is the duration of Q waves in lead aVF of the standard ECG. Figure 2.7 shows that there are two separate groups of patients. The group that is delineated by the upper vertical arrow is the group of normal patients. The group that is indicated by the lower vertical arrow is the group of patients with inferior MI. The total number of patients depicted in Figure 2.7 is 862 and consists of 497 normal patients and 365 patients with inferior MI. The data shown in this vertical display are the encoded Z scores of the lead aVF Q wave durations that had been recorded in milliseconds.

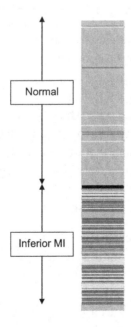

Fig. 2.7. Q wave durations in lead aVF. Normal versus inferior MI subgroups.

In the compressed colored Z score display shown in Figure 2.7, the gray portions indicate the patients whose lead aVF Q wave durations are not statistically significantly different from normal. A color screen or printout of this display would show yellow, orange, and red portions that would indicate the patients whose lead aVF Q wave durations are statistically significantly greater than normal (P values <0.05, <0.01, and <0.001, respectively). The thick, black horizontal line in the display is used in Figure 2.7 to show the demarcation between the normal and the inferior MI groups. Thus, Figure 2.7 shows that a compressed, encoded display of Z scores can permit one to identify important abnormalities very quickly and accurately even in a large amount of data – in this case, important ECG findings in 862 different patients. Needless to say, it would have taken much longer to examine lead aVF Q wave durations one ECG at a time.

To produce compressed displays such as those in Figures 2.6 and 2.7, first highlight all the rows in the spreadsheet that you want to compress. Then, follow the above instructions for showing the row height. Next replace the number "12.75" with the number "1" in the rows that have been highlighted. The highlighted rows will then compress to produce a display similar to those shown in Figures 2.6 and 2.7.

There are several advantages to showing color-coded Z scores using spreadsheet rows that have been compressed in this way. First, the compression of the row heights makes the most efficient use of the space on any screen or printout paper. Second, showing a large amount of data in a small space increases the efficiency with which one can review all data that have been generated. Third, being able to see many data points at the same time can reveal patterns in the data that otherwise might not have been noticed. By analogy, a television screen that shows a large number of illuminated pixels provides a much more meaningful set of patterns than does long series of screens that show a much smaller number of pixels at a time.

Compressing spreadsheet rows in this way prevents one from directly seeing the actual numbers in the spreadsheet's cells. However, this is not an important problem for several reasons. First, as Figures 2.6 and 2.7 show, colors that would indicate statistically significant Z scores are easily seen. This demonstrates a major advantage of color-coding over just displaying the data as numbers. For example, a color-coded display would easily show a change from gray to colored in Figure 2.6, the transition between nonsignificant and significant Z score data. Second, by clicking on a part of the display that contains either verbal or numerical information, the formula bar at the top of the screen immediately reveals the contents of the cell on which you have clicked. Third, one can easily uncompress the rows in any area of interest on the display by simply changing the row height back to 12.75 for that region of the display.

To further increase the amount of color-coded Z score data shown on a screen or a printout, one can also decrease the width of the columns that contain the color-coded data. Simply highlight the columns that you wish to make narrower, right click on the letter above any one of the highlighted columns, and then enter the desired width of the highlight columns in the popup window.

Obviously, it's easy to combine the processes of row compression and column narrowing to maximize the amount of data that one can display on a screen or printout. For example, one can enter sequential color-coded Z score data into adjacent columns in a spreadsheet, compress the rows containing the data to one unit, and narrow the columns to a desired width. The color-coded data would then be examined from top to bottom in each of the columns and then moved on to the adjacent column. If one wanted to add headings to any of the columns, one could add an uncompressed row above the compressed columns of data and enter the headings in this top row.

In addition to spreadsheet software, many statistical programs have modules that calculate Z scores. For example, the statistics program IBM SPSS® has a module that calculates Z scores extremely quickly. To do this, use the following steps:

1. In an open file of the data you wish to analyze, left click "Analyze" at the top of the page.
2. Left click "Descriptives" in the pop-up window.
3. In the next pop-up window, choose in the left panel all the parameters for which you wish the Z scores to be calculated, and then left click on them.
4. Next, left click on the black arrow that points to the right panel entitled "Variable(s)." This will move the parameters for which you have chosen Z scores to be calculated.

5. Then, by performing any of the several operations listed under "Analyze," the Z scores will be calculated.
6. In the "Variable" view, the parameters for which the Z scores have just been calculated will appear under the list of all the original variables. The name of each newly calculated Z score variable will begin with a small z, followed by the original variable's name.

It is important to note that calculating Z scores with IBM SPSS using the above steps, employs the mean and SD of the original set of data for each parameter. In other words, it compares the data points to the mean of the same population to which they belong. However, one can also use this program to calculate the Z scores using either the mean of a database of known normals or to the mean of a database that represents a baseline condition. One uses this statistical program to calculate the mean and SD of any population of data that is desired for comparison and then uses this mean and SD to calculate the Z scores. To do this:

1. Left click "Transform" at the top of the page.
2. Left click "Compute Variable" in the pop-up window.
3. Name the Target Variable, e.g., "Z_Score_Age."
4. Enter the formula (Variable Name − Mean)/SD.
5. In the data view, you will now have a column of Z scores for the variable that you have chosen.

The formula for calculating Z scores shows that it involves nothing more simple arithmetic calculations involving three easily obtainable numbers – a recorded data point and the mean and the SD of a reference population of data. As has been shown above, it is very easy to calculate and display Z scores on a personal computer or similar device using widely available, off-the-shelf software with which many readers are already familiar. Furthermore, the same ease of using Z scores would also readily permit programmers to adapt them for use on other platforms such as medical monitors, seismographs, electronic tablets, and smart phones.

The use of Z scores is by no means confined to the review and interpretation of biomedical data. The diversity of the applications in which Z scores can be used will now be illustrated by describing their use in such dissimilar activities as personal investing and the analysis of seismological data by geologists.

USING Z SCORES IN PERSONAL INVESTING

Z scores can be used in various ways to help evaluate information that is important to personal investors. One reason for this is that the Internet now provides a very large amount of information about investment vehicles such as stocks, bonds, exchange trade funds, and mutual funds. Furthermore, much of this information regarding possible investments is updated frequently. Consequently, investors face the task of interpreting diverse, abundant, and rapidly changing information. Access to data relevant to investing sometimes requires the investor to purchase a membership in the organization that provides the financial information. However, a great deal of this information is also available on various websites at no cost. Furthermore, the proliferation of financial sites on the Internet enables investors to buy and sell stocks, bonds, etc. at very low transaction costs compared to the fees charged by full service brokers. Of course, the avoidance of brokerage fees entails the risk of making investment decisions in the absence of professional advice. These factors further increase the importance to investors of having especially efficient and accurate methods for analyzing the data that are now available to them.

There are at least two important ways in which using Z scores can increase the likelihood that an investor is successful. One way is to help the investor decide *which* investment to purchase and the other is to help the investor decide *when* to buy and sell it. The next two subsections of this chapter will discuss methods that address each of these decisions.

It is to be emphasized that it is not the intent of the author to provide investment advice to anyone. Instead, this section of the chapter merely describes methods for examining financial data that individuals may wish to evaluate if they are making investment decisions with or without the help of investment professionals.

Choosing Which Stock, Bond, or Fund to Buy

One way in which an investor can use Z scores is to help the investor choose exactly which specific security he or she should buy. This choice typically involves picking securities such as stocks, bonds, or funds that are especially likely to increase in price in the relatively near future so that the investor can "buy low and sell high." The choice of security may also involve determining which stock, bond, or fund pays the highest dividends or interest during the period in which the investor holds the security. The decision about which security to purchase may also involve the assessment of how much it costs (in addition to the actual price of the security itself) to buy the security. These costs to the investor may include brokerage fees, recurring annual fees charged by an investment company, front-end loads that are charged when the security is purchased, back-end loads that are assessed when the security is sold, and expenses that an investment company charges to cover the company's administrative costs. These administrative costs that are paid by investors are often expressed as a security's "expense ratio," which represents the ratio of the administrative costs to the dollar value of the assets under management. Needless to say, it advisable for an investor to try to minimize the costs of buying, holding, and selling an investment. This is because the lower these costs are, the greater is the proportion of the money generated by price appreciation and the distributions of capital gains, dividends, and interest that the investor is able to keep.

Choosing which stock, bond or fund to purchase is a daunting task, partly because of the very large number of securities among which the investor must choose. For example, there are thousands of mutual funds that various investment companies offer for sale to investors. Furthermore, there are many different quantifiable parameters by which stocks, bonds, and funds can be evaluated and compared. Fortunately, computerized data that are highly relevant to the selection of various securities are available to personal investors and investment professionals at many different websites.

Table 2.6 shows how Z scores can help an investor select a specific mutual fund. For the purposes of this example, let us say that the investor decides to buy a mutual fund that has an especially high year-to-date return, a low expense ratio, and a relatively large amount of assets under management. Considering only the raw data relevant to these three parameters typically raises the questions of, "How high should be considered to be high, and how low should be considered to be low?" Using Z scores rather than just the raw data enables the investor to ask questions that are much easier to answer in an objective, unbiased way: "Of the mutual funds that are available for purchase, are there any whose year-to-date returns and assets under management are statistically

Table 2.6 Examples of Using Z Scores to Select Mutual Funds

Fund #	YTD Return (%)	Exp. Ratio (%)	Assets ($ Million)	Fund #	YTD Return (%)	Exp. Ratio (%)	Assets ($ Million)	Fund #	YTD Return (%)	Exp. Ratio (%)	Assets ($ Million)
1	3.93	0.88	4	47	−9.39	1.5	3	93	3.32	0.97	184
2	3.93	0.88	4	48	0.99	1.4	161	94	3.32	0.97	184
3	4.02	0.58	4	49	0.99	1.4	161	95	3.49	0.67	184
4	4.02	1.58	4	50	0.61	2.15	161	96	3.07	1.67	184
5	3.83	0.58	4	51	1.09	1.15	161	97	3	1.67	184
6	3.78	0.9	30	52	−0.32	0.99	28	98	3.5	0.67	184
7	3.78	1.1	30	53	−0.32	0.99	28	99	3.39	0.92	184
8	3.88	0.63	30	54	−0.65	1.74	28	100	3.31	1.17	184
9	3.88	0.97	30	55	−0.22	0.74	28	101	3.8	0.99	189
10	3.67	1.13	30	56	1.03	0.63	52	102	3.8	0.99	189
11	2	0.92	10	57	1.03	0.88	52	103	3.97	0.69	189
12	2	1.69	10	58	0.79	1.58	52	104	3.5	1.69	189
13	2.1	0.9	10	59	1.21	0.9	52	105	3.51	1.69	189
14	2.1	0.63	10	60	2.86	1.58	53	106	3.88	0.69	189
15	1.9	0.88	10	61	1.33	0.82	7	107	3.88	0.94	189
16	4.74	1.75	455	62	1.33	0.82	7	108	3.69	1.19	189
17	4.74	1.75	455	63	1.52	0.52	7	109	4.3	1.01	157
18	4.41	2.5	455	64	1.04	1.52	7	110	4.3	1.01	157
19	4.81	1.5	455	65	1.07	1.52	7	111	4.55	0.71	157
20	3.37	1.12	6	66	1.4	0.52	7	112	3.99	1.71	157
21	2.08	1.25	11	67	1.4	0.77	7	113	4	1.71	157
22	2.08	1.25	11	68	1.29	1.02	7	114	4.57	0.71	157
23	1.78	2	11	69	2.09	0.88	8	115	4.38	0.96	157
24	2.19	1	11	70	2.09	0.88	8	116	4.19	1.21	157
25	1.86	1.44	110	71	2.19	0.58	8	117	4.77	1.01	128
26	1.58	2.11	110	72	1.73	1.58	8	118	4.77	1.01	128
27	2.05	1.06	110	73	1.75	1.58	8	119	4.85	0.71	128
28	0.27	0.75	142	74	2.22	0.58	8	120	4.44	1.71	128
29	0.27	0.75	142	75	2.12	0.83	8	121	4.38	1.71	128
30	0.03	1.3	142	76	1.99	1.08	8	122	4.87	0.71	128
31	0.39	0.6	142	77	2.52	0.9	49	123	4.77	0.96	128
32	1.09	1.23	134	78	2.52	0.9	49	124	4.6	1.21	128
33	1.09	1.23	134	79	2.61	0.6	49	125	5.09	1.02	112
34	0.71	2.43	134	80	2.25	1.6	49	126	5.09	1.02	112
35	0.8	1.92	134	81	2.18	1.6	49	127	5.24	0.72	112

(Continued)

Table 2.6 Examples of Using Z Scores to Select Mutual Funds *(cont.)*

Fund #	YTD Return (%)	Exp. Ratio (%)	Assets ($ Million)	Fund #	YTD Return (%)	Exp. Ratio (%)	Assets ($ Million)	Fund #	YTD Return (%)	Exp. Ratio (%)	Assets ($ Million)
36	1.16	0.97	134	82	2.62	0.6	49	128	4.69	1.72	112
37	0.5	1.1	29	83	2.52	0.85	49	129	4.7	1.72	112
38	0.4	0.58	29	84	2.42	1.1	49	130	5.21	0.72	112
39	0.59	0.97	29	85	2.99	0.93	103	131	5.04	0.97	112
40	−2.33	1.97	18	86	2.99	0.93	103	132	4.93	1.22	112
41	−2.54	2.22	18	87	3.16	0.63	103	133	5.09	1.02	88
42	4.55	2	18	88	2.73	1.63	103	134	5.09	1.02	88
43	4.47	2.24	18	89	2.66	1.95	103	135	5.18	0.72	88
44	7.78	1.79	784	90	3.17	0.63	103	136	4.8	1.72	88
45	7.66	2.03	784	91	3.06	0.88	103	137	4.73	1.72	88
46	−9.35	1.25	3	92	2.88	1.13	103	138	5.25	0.72	88

Exp., expense; YTD, year-to-date.

significantly greater than the rest and any whose expense ratios are statistically significantly lower than the rest?"

For the purpose of illustration, Table 2.6 shows relevant data on 138 different mutual funds, each of which is designated by a number in the first column of each of the table's vertical panels. In each of the panels, the remaining columns show each fund's year-to-date returns, the expense ratios, and the value of the assets under management. These investment data were downloaded from a free financial website. This website contained data relevant to many different parameters for thousands of funds, but only 138 are used in Table 2.6 for purposes of illustration. Also, on that website, the tables of data contained the funds' actual names, rather than the numbers one through 138 shown here. After downloading the data included in Table 2.6, the author used an Excel spreadsheet to calculate the means and SDs of each of the three parameters shown Table 2.6. He then used these means and SDs to calculate the Z scores of each value of the three parameters. Each value of any of the parameter whose Z score is >1.65 ($P < 0.05$) was then colored orange (using the conditional formatting function of Excel) and each value of any parameter whose Z score is <−1.65 ($P < 0.05$) was colored blue.

A color-coded display based on the statistical significance of the calculated Z scores would make the investment data in Table 2.6 especially easy to analyze. For example, Fund #40 and Fund #41 exhibit the undesirable combination of a significantly low year-to-date return and a significantly high expense ratio. In contrast, Fund #44 and Fund #45 would show significantly higher year-to-date returns and significantly more assets under management than the average of the 138 funds listed in Table 2.6. However, using this hypothetical investor's criteria for selection, Table 2.6 suggests that Fund #44 is superior to Fund #45 as a security in which to invest. This is because Fund #45, but not Fund #44, also has a significantly higher expense ratio than the average of all the funds.

Since spreadsheet software accommodates a large amount of data and also enables one to calculate Z scores very rapidly, one easily can generate much larger tables of relevant financial data than Table 2.6 shows. Furthermore, color-coding would permit one to identify statistically significant values of these data very quickly, even when many pages of data must be reviewed.

Deciding When to Buy and When to Sell an Investment
As discussed in the previous section of this chapter, it is important to choose a stock, bond, or fund whose value is especially likely to increase in the relatively near future. Therefore, an additional fundamental goal of investing is to try to determine the optimal times to buy and subsequently sell a security so that one can make a profit with these transactions. Obviously, the general goal is to buy a security when its price is relatively low and then sell it when its price is relatively high. Unfortunately, predicting the future direction and amount of the changes in a security's price, even in the short term, is highly uncertain. However, because of the statistical principles underlying their use, Z scores may be able to diminish that uncertainty and correspondingly increase the confidence with which an investor can choose the times to purchase and then sell securities.

Figure 2.8 shows a technical chart, in this case a line graph, of the daily closing prices over a period of approximately 1 year of one of the 30 stocks that make up the Dow Jones Industrial Index. In Figure 2.8, the heavy black line shows the actual closing prices and these prices begin on the left on June 2, 2014 and end on the right on May 29, 2015.

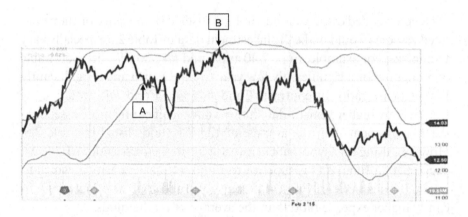

Fig. 2.8. Technical chart with Z score lines.

In addition, a pair of thinner gray lines surrounds the line graph of the closing prices. These thinner lines are graphical depictions of Z scores because they represent a particular number of SDs above and below, respectively, the mean of a trailing moving average of the security's closing prices. For example, a 50-day trailing moving average of a security's closing prices on a given day consists of the arithmetic mean of all the security's daily closing prices on each of the preceding 50 trading days. The SD that is also needed to calculate the Z scores of the security's closing prices is computed using the same 50 prices.

In the example shown in Figure 2.8, the Z score lines represent two SDs above and below the value of a 50-day trailing moving average. Investors may use these Z score lines to assess the volatility of a security's price. The amount of volatility exhibited by the security's prices is proportional to the distance between the upper and lower Z score lines. Since Figure 2.8 shows the distance between the upper and lower Z score lines changed during the year, one can infer that the volatility of this security's prices varied during the same period.

However, because of the properties of Z scores, investors can use these lines in another important way. As stated above, the Z score lines in Figure 2.8 are two SDs above and below the 50-day trailing moving average of this stock's closing prices. A distance from the mean of two SDs is associated with a statistical P value of 0.023. This means that the probability of the closing price of this stock on a particular day falling two SDs below its 50-day moving average is only 0.023, i.e., one chance in 44. Similarly, there is only one chance in 44 that the stock's closing price on a particular day will exceed the 50-day moving average two SDs.

Arrow A in Figure 2.8 shows a point during a particular period at which the stock's closing price first intersects the lower Z score line, and Arrow B shows the point at which the closing price subsequently intersects the upper Z score line. Since reaching either of these points is statistically improbable with respect to the stock's prices of the past 50 days, Arrow A suggests a point at which the stock is in an relatively "oversold" condition and is quite unlikely to fall much further in the immediate future. By similar reasoning, Arrow B suggests a point at which the stock is in an "overbought" condition and is statistically unlikely to rise much further in a similar period. Needless to say, a compelling investment strategy is to buy a security when its price is relatively low and unlikely to fall further in the near term and then to sell it when the security's price rises to a level that it is unlikely to exceed in the near future.

One can assess the advantage of using this strategy involving the Z score lines by comparing it to the "buy and hold" strategy commonly employed by investors. For purposes of this comparison, the "buy and hold" strategy is exemplified by buying 1000 shares of this stock at the beginning of the year and then selling these shares at the end of the year. The Z score line method in this case consists buying 1000 shares of the stock at Point A of Figure 2.8 and then selling the shares at Point B.

Table 2.7 shows that if the investor had bought 1000 shares of this stock at Point A and sold it 65 days later when it reached Point B, she

Table 2.7 Investing Using the Z Score Method Versus Buy and Hold 1000 Shares of Stock

		Date	Price per Share	Value	$ per Day
Z Score	Purchase	9/22/14	$15.83	$15,830	
	Sale	11/26/14	$17.60	$17,600	
	Difference	65 days	$1.77	$1,770	$27.23
Buy and Hold	Purchase	6/2/14	$13.83	$13,830	
	Sale	5/29/15	$12.50	$12,500	
	Difference	361 days	$-1.33	-$1,330	-$3.68

would have made a profit of $1770, or $27.23 per day. Conversely, if she had bought the same stock in late May of 2014 and held it for approximately 1 year, she would have *lost* $1330, or $3.68 per day. Certainly, the total amount of money either gained or lost by the investor, using either the Z score method or the buy and hold strategy, is highly important. Also important, however, is the amount of time during which an investment is held. This is because of a phenomenon known as the opportunity cost of investing. This involves the observation that whatever money is tied up in one investment is not available for other investments that could possibly be even more profitable. In the buy and hold strategy shown in Table 2.7, the $13,830 needed to buy 1,000 shares of the stock would have been tied up for approximately a year and therefore not available for any other kind of investment or even a certificate of deposit or a savings account. Using the Z score method, however, $15,830 required to buy 1,000 shares of the stock on September 22, 2014 would have been tied up for only 65 days. Upon selling the shares on November 26, 2014, the investor would have had $17,600 available for other investments or for savings accounts, depending upon what he or she chose to do with the money.

USING Z SCORES IN GEOLOGY

Z scores can facilitate the analysis of data in numerous fields, including the physical, biological, and behavioral sciences. This is illustrated by the possible use of Z scores in geology.

An important part of the science of geology is seismology – the study of data provided by instruments that are used to detect earthquakes. These instruments are called seismographs, and they produce records of data concerning episodes of shaking of the earth's crust that are called seismograms. There are numerous seismographs placed all over the earth, including on the bottoms of the oceans. For example, the Global Seismographic Network consists of more than 150 stations that record digital seismographic data from over 80 countries [10]. An important goal of seismology is the prediction of earthquakes in the hope that people in the area of an impending earthquake will have sufficient time to take action to avoid injury and loss of life. The basis for efforts to predict earthquakes is that they are often preceded by "foreshock swarms" of seismic activity characterized by recorded vibrations of relatively high amplitude and frequency. Z scores might assist efforts to predict the occurrence of earthquakes in the following ways:

1. *Provide Objective, Statistically Meaningful Information About Seismograms* – Z scores would provide objective evidence that the amplitudes and frequencies (and therefore the total energy) of episodes of seismic activity are statistically significantly greater than the baseline activity recorded by the seismographs. This objective evidence of greater intensity of seismic activity could give more reliable evidence of an impending damaging earthquake than more subjective evaluations of the seismographic data are likely to provide. Figure 2.9 illustrates how Z scores might augment an analog display of seismological data. Figure 2.9 shows an isolated high-amplitude seismic impulse followed by a series of high-amplitude, high-frequency seismic movements. On a color screen or printout, a blue and violet horizontal bar near the top of the display would indicate that this series of seismic movements exhibited statistically significantly short cycle lengths, i.e., were of abnormally increased frequency compared to the baseline condition. A lower series of yellow, orange, and red bars would

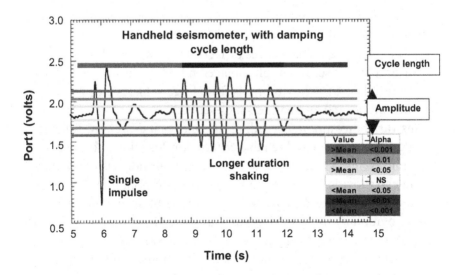

Fig. 2.9. Z scores for evaluating seismic activity.

show that the amplitudes of the same seismic displacements were also of statistically significantly greater amplitude than the baseline condition. Such a combination of significant increases in both the frequency and amplitude of seismic activity suggests that the likelihood of an impending earthquake is increased.

2. *Normalize for Differences in Recording Characteristics of Individual Devices* – The ability to calculate the Z scores using the means and the SDs of the baseline data for each seismograph is especially important. This is because the data recorded by the seismographs can vary considerably from device to device. There are several possible reasons for this lack of uniformity:

 a. Although manufacturers and users of each seismograph attempt to calibrate the device in conformance with uniform standards, the sensitivities of the individual seismographs may change, e.g., with time alone or as a result of some degree of damage to the devices.

 b. There are differences in the proximities of the nearby recorders to the fault lines that are the sources of the seismic events. Longer distances between the event and the recorder tend to lower the amplitudes of the seismographic data.

 c. The nature of the ground on which the seismographs are placed is variable. Placing the device on or near bedrock will tend to attenuate seismic vibrations. Conversely, placing the device on looser soil will tend to amplify the vibrations.

 d. There may be other sources of recorded vibration. For example, if a seismograph is placed relatively close to a highway or a railroad track, vibrations from large vehicles may be misinterpreted as small seismic events.

This variability among recording sites makes it especially difficult to develop uniform and reliable criteria for detecting and predicting seismic events. The use of Z scores rather than raw seismographic data can provide a solution to this problem of nonuniformity. One could calculate the Z scores for the records obtained from each seismograph by using the baseline data recorded by that same device. This would automatically normalize for any variations in device characteristics, proximity, nonseismic vibrations, and the nature of the ground on which the device is placed. The resultant Z scores would then show whether any recorded vibration differed statistically significantly from each device's location-specific baseline condition.

3. *Permit Meaningful Comparisons of the Different Types of Seismic Waves* – There are multiple types of seismic waves recorded by seismographs, and these include primary, secondary, Rayleigh, and Love waves. Displaying these waves as graphs of Z scores rather than as graphs of the raw data will show them on the same scale and thereby facilitate meaningful comparisons among them.

4. *Facilitate the Development of Criteria for Predicting Earthquakes* – The advantages of converting seismological data to Z scores may make it easier to improve the accuracy with which earthquakes can be predicted. The methods for doing this would be analogous

November 2011									
CL									
Ampl.									
1	2	3	4	5	6	7	8	9	10
Nov.	Nov.	Nov.	Nov.	Nov.	Nov.	Nov.	Nov.	Nov.	Nov.
CL									
Ampl.									
11	12	13	14	15	16	17	18	19	20
Nov.	Nov.	Nov.	Nov.	Nov.	Nov.	Nov.	Nov.	Nov.	Nov.
CL									
Ampl.									
21	22	23	24	25	26	27	28	29	30
Nov.	Nov.	Nov.	Nov.	Nov.	Nov.	Nov.	Nov.	Nov.	Nov.

November 24, 2011								
CL								
Ampl.								
MN	1	2	3	4	5	6	7	8
	am	am	am	am	am	am	am	am
CL								
Ampl.								
9	10	11	Noon	1	2	3	4	5
am	am	am		pm	pm	pm	pm	pm
CL								
Ampl.								
6	7	8	10	11	MN			
pm	pm	pm	pm	pm				

Fig. 2.10. Rapid review of seismological data.

to developing optimal medical diagnostic criteria for a particular disease, as was illustrated earlier in this chapter. One could use two groups of normalized recorded seismological data. In one group, the recorded seismic events preceded an actual earthquake. In the other group, an earthquake did not follow the recorded events. Both groups of data could then be used to develop objective, uniform criteria that exhibit the best sensitivities and specificities for predicting impending and potentially damaging earthquakes.

Once the optimal seismological parameters for predicting earthquakes have been determined, it will be necessary to have meaningful and efficient ways to display them. This is because the numerous seismographs throughout the world continuously collect data that must be reviewed. Figure 2.10 shows a way of displaying the Z scores of the seismic data in such a way that the information can be very quickly examined. The color-coding of Z scores in the upper panels of Figure 2.10 would show each day in a particular month in which occurred seismic activity characterized by statistically significantly shorter cycle lengths and/or statistically significantly increased amplitudes for a particular seismograph. A colored display would show that the most abnormal combination of cycle length and amplitude occurred on November 24. The lower panel exhibits the data on a smaller time scale and shows more detailed information for that particular day. Thus, the use of color-coded Z scores in this way provides a scalable method for identifying and analyzing abnormal seismic activity.

REFERENCES

[1] Berger JO, Strawderman WE. Choice of hierarchical priors: admissibility in estimation of normal means. Ann Stat 1996;24(3):931–51.

[2] Warner RA. Color-coded z scores for the display and analysis of biomedical data. 2nd World Congress on Biomarkers and Clinical Research. J Mol Biomark Diagn 2011;2(4):33.

[3] Warner RA. Using standardized numerical scores for the display and interpretation of biomedical data. In: Arabnia HR, Tran Q, editors. Advances in Experimental Medicine and Biology (Software Tools and Algorithms for Biological Systems). New York: Springer; 2010. p. 725–31.

[4] Barnard W. JURAN Institute's Six Sigma Breakthrough and Beyond – quality performance breakthrough methods. New York: Tata McGraw-Hill Publishing Company Limited; 2005.

[5] Warner RA, Olicker AL, Haisty WK, Hill NE, Selvester RH, Wagner GS. The importance of accounting for the variability of electrocardiographic data among diagnostically similar patients. Am J Cardiol 2000;86:1238–40.

[6] Hill NE, Warner RA, Mookherjee S, Smulyan H. Comparison of optimal scalar electrocardiographic orthogonal electrocardiographic and vectorcardiographic criteria for diagnosing inferior and, anterior MI. Am J Cardiol 1984;14:274–6.

[7] Marcus GM, Gerber IL, McKeown BH, Vessey JC, Jordan MV, Huddleston M, McCulloch CE, Foster E, Chatterjee K, Michaels AD. Association between phonocardiographic third and fourth heart sounds and objective measures of left ventricular function. JAMA 2005;293(18):2238–44.

[8] Zuber M, Kipfer P, Attenhofer Jost CH. Usefulness of acoustic cardiography to resolve ambiguous values of B-type natriuretic peptide levels in patients with suspected heart failure. Am J Cardiol 2007;100(5):866–9.

[9] Warner RA, Hill NE. Optimized electrocardiographic criteria for prior inferior and an anterior MI. J Electrocardiol 2012;45:209–13.

[10] Gee, L.S., Leith, W.S., 2011. The Global Seismographic Network: U.S. Geological Survey Fact Sheet 2011-3021.

CHAPTER 3

Moving Averages for Identifying Trends and Changes in the Data

TIME SERIES OF DATA AND CLUSTERED EVENTS

An important task that is often associated with the use of information is the evaluation of time series of data. A time series is a collection of data in which the individual values of the data points change over time. An example of a time series is a set of data that shows the changes in the daily closing prices of a stock that have occurred during the past 5 years. Another example is a recording of the minute-to-minute changes in a hospitalized patient's recorded blood pressure during an 8-h period. The general purpose of analyzing time series of data is to detect events of interest that may have occurred during the period of data collection. Once these events have been detected, further analysis of the time series may show meaningful patterns related to the timing of these events both in isolation and in relation to one another.

In using time series of data to detect and study events of interest, it is important to choose intervals of time for recording the data that are appropriate for the particular event. This choice depends on the event's expected duration and the frequency with which it is likely to occur. For example, if each occurrence of the event of interest is expected to persist for several seconds and may occur a few times every minute, then selecting an entire day for the recording interval would be inappropriate. This is because such a recording interval is too long to meaningfully display events of such short duration and high frequency. A large disparity between the actual frequency of an event and the frequency with which it has been recorded provides little or no useful information about the event. Such a mismatch between data frequency and recording frequency is related to the problem of "aliasing" in engineering. Aliasing occurs when the rate at which data are presented to a recording device is greater than the speed with which the device can record the data. This is often seen in movies when the wheels of a rapidly moving vehicle appear to unexpectedly change speeds and even reverse direction, despite the fact that the velocity of the vehicle itself does not change. This phenomenon occurs because the speed with which the vehicle's wheels are actually rotating exceeds the speed with which the movie camera can record the rotation.

In time series of data that have been compiled using appropriate frequencies of recording, the display of the data shows that each of the detected events of interest is extended in time, i.e., has a measurable duration. This means that the recorded values of the data that are used to reveal each occurrence of the event of interest are temporally clustered. For example, each tremor associated with an earthquake does not suddenly appear and then immediately vanish. Instead, the seismographic evidence for earthquakes shows that each tremor persists for an observable period, i.e., the evidence for the tremor is clustered with respect to time. In geology, these clusters are called "swarms" of seismic activity. Clustering of this type is also highly typical of biological events. The physiology of humans and other organisms does not permit changes in their conditions to instantaneously appear and disappear. Instead, changes in a particular physiological condition have easily measurable durations. Therefore, the numerical values of the measurements used to detect these physiological changes appear as clusters in the data used to detect them. These clusters represent measurements that differ from the measurements associated with the baseline condition.

The following is an operational definition of a clustered event:

1. The event is extended in time.
2. The event tends to change the measurable values of at least one parameter in a directionally consistent way. Some events of interest increase the measured values of the parameters used to detect them. Other events tend to decrease the values of their associated parameters. However, the same type of event tends not to alternately increase and decrease the values of the same parameter.
3. The duration of the changes in the parameter(s) exceeds the sampling interval of the data that reflect these changes. If this were not the case, the equivalent of aliasing would occur.

The specific features of clusters of data can themselves also provide important information. This is because various characteristics of events of interest are often well known.

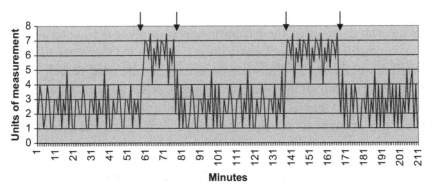

Fig. 3.1. Line graph of a clustered event.

Figure 3.1 illustrates two clustered events of different duration in a line graph of data. The vertical black arrows mark the beginning and end of each of the clusters. As shown on the graph's X-axis, the time over which the data were acquired and recorded is expressed in minutes. The Y-axis shows the values of the units of measurement that were used to quantify the changes in the parameter over time. The entire graph reveals considerable sample-to-sample variation in the recorded values of the data points. In the clusters, this variation continues, but the data points in the clusters tend to have greater recorded values than the data points before and after the clusters.

One of the important characteristics of a clustered event is its duration. Therefore, in analyzing time series of relevant data to detect the occurrence of an event, the durations of the clusters of the data should be consistent with the known range of durations of that event. For example, if a patient is hospitalized because of chest pain, she might be monitored to try to detect ECG evidence that her chest pain is due to heart disease. During the period of monitoring, it is noted that clusters of suspicious-looking ECG abnormalities occur. It is also observed that each of these clusters of ECG abnormalities persists for only for a few seconds. This observation about the duration of the clusters is important because it is known that episodes of chest pain due to heart disease characteristically last for at least several minutes rather than for only a few seconds. Therefore, despite their qualitative appearance, clusters of ECG abnormalities of such short duration are likely to be due to some condition other than heart disease. In fact, because many medical and non-medical events of interest have a characteristic range of durations, the measured values of these durations can sometimes be used as additional quantitative criteria for detecting the event. At the very least, such information about the durations of events can be used to help determine the prior probability that an event of interest has occurred. As will be discussed in Chapter 7, estimating prior probabilities can greatly increase the accuracy of conclusions that result from the analysis of data.

PRESERVING INFORMATION WHILE REDUCING ARTIFACT

A major challenge in analyzing time series of data consists of distinguishing meaningful clusters of data from artifacts. A way to address this problem is to "smooth" the data that are being reviewed. By doing this, it is hoped that the magnitude of random fluctuations in the data will decrease. This, in turn, could make it easier for genuine data clusters associated with the events of interest to stand out and be easier to distinguish from the baseline data that surround them. However, techniques for smoothing recorded data inevitably involve altering the data in some way. Therefore, any method that one uses to smooth data is constrained by the need to preserve as much useful information as possible. Improving the appearance of displays of data to facilitate their review should not come at the cost of reducing the accuracy with which the data can be interpreted.

A method that has been used to smooth data in time series is to calculate and display trailing moving averages of the data [1–3]. In calculating trailing moving averages for a set of data, it is first necessary to select the number of recorded raw data points to include in the calculation. For example, consider a database that consists of the daily closing price of a stock during a 12-month period and for which we choose to calculate the 10-day trailing moving average during that entire period. Each value of the 10-day trailing moving average consists of the numerical average of the stock's daily closing prices for the preceding, i.e., "trailing," 10 trading days. In this example, the first 10-day trailing moving average would be calculated for day 11 of the total time of collection and consist of the averages of all the values of the data that had been recorded on trading days one through 10. The second average would be calculated for day 12 and would consist of the averages of all the values of the data that had been recorded on days two through 11. This process is then repeated for every stock-trading day during the remainder of the 12-month period.

It is important to clarify exactly what is meant by the word "average." In the analysis of data, average is a measure of central tendency. It is a way of very roughly summarizing the magnitude of the measured values of the data points in an entire set of recorded data. There are several different types of averages, and these are the ones that are most commonly used:

1. Mean (or arithmetic mean) – This is what is most commonly meant when the word "average" is used. It consists of the sum of all the values in a set of data divided by the number of data points in that set.
2. Mode – This is the most commonly-occurring value in a set of data.
3. Median – When all the data points in a set of data are arranged in either ascending or descending order, the median is the value that is at the midpoint of this arrangement. In other words, the median is the value in a set of data that has an equal number of data points whose values are above and below it.

Unless specified otherwise, the calculation of a trailing moving average involves using the arithmetic mean of the data.

In evaluating data, it is important to be able to distinguish between signal and noise, and moving averages are sometimes used to do this. A signal differs from noise in that the former conveys meaningful information, and the latter does not. Engineers commonly encounter this problem when they use electronic band pass filters to alter signals. For example, an electronic filter for devices used for music should eliminate unwelcome noise in the sound signal, but not significantly impair the quality of the music being played.

A famous example of the importance of distinguishing signal from noise occurred in 1964 when two physicists named Arno Penzias and Robert Wilson were using a highly sensitive antenna to try to detect faint radio waves. The physicists were troubled by the presence of what they had initially attributed to low intensity background noise. However, further work revealed that it was not noise at all, but something far more significant. Instead, what they had initially believed to be meaningless noise actually represented the uniform background cosmic microwave radiation that has provided strong evidentiary support for the Big Bang theory of the origin of the universe [4].

CHOOSING THE DURATIONS OF MOVING AVERAGES

Obviously, the greater the length of the trailing period that one selects, the greater is the number of data points that are used to calculate the moving average. It is also true that the greater the length of the trailing period, the greater is the amount of data smoothing that occurs. This is because a moving average that has been calculated using a large number of points will be less influenced by an unusually high or low value of a single data point than will an average that has been calculated using a smaller amount of data. In other words, the greater the number of data points that have been used to calculate a moving average, the less that average will be diluted by a given large or small value. Figure 3.2 illustrates this point. The thin light gray line shows the recorded closing prices of a stock for each day of trading during a 2-year period. The closing price of the stock in dollars is on the vertical axis and the day on which the price was recorded is on the horizontal axis. The thick light gray line represents the 50-day trailing moving average and thick dark gray line is the 10-day trailing moving average.

Figure 3.2 shows that the line that exhibits the greatest amount of day-to-day variation is the thin light gray line that represents the stock's recorded daily prices. The 10-day trailing moving average shown by the thick dark gray line shows less fluctuation than the daily prices themselves. The thick light gray line that reveals the stock's 50-day trailing

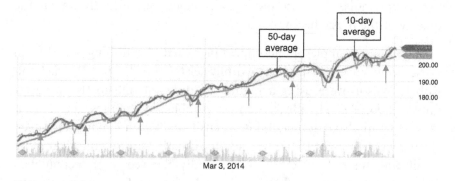

Fig. 3.2. Stock price chart with moving averages.

moving average shows the least daily fluctuation of the three lines. Figure 3.2 shows that both the 10-day and the 50-day trailing moving averages smooth the price data. However, the 50-day average produces more smoothing than does the 10-day average because of the greater number of recorded data points that had been used to calculate it.

A useful way to think of the analog display of data in Figure 3.2 is as an intuitive method of both detecting and characterizing trends in a set of sequential data. If Figure 3.1 showed only the actual closing prices of the stock, one could correctly conclude that there was a generally upward trend in the stock's prices during the 2-year period during which the closing prices were recorded. However, the use of moving averages of different trailing periods provides additional information that is both important and easily discernible. Like the stock's prices themselves, both the 10-day and the 50-day trailing moving averages show generally upward trends. However, during the 2-year period, there are at least eight separate occasions when the 10-day moving average clearly rises faster than the 50-day moving average. The upwardly pointing arrows mark the onsets of each of these occasions. Figure 3.2 shows that each of these points of divergence between the two moving averages marks the beginning of a period of when the stock's price rises. The above pattern suggests that at each of the eight points of divergence of the two moving averages, there was at least one circumstance that favorably influenced the short-term performance of the stock compared to its longer-term performance. It is also important to note that after each of the points of divergence of the moving averages shown by the vertical arrows, the 10-day trailing moving average did not begin to converge with the 50-day trailing moving average for several days or weeks. These observations suggest the possibility that buying a stock at the beginning of each divergence and then selling it at the onset of its subsequent convergence may be a profitable strategy. In the parlance of investing, the onset of the divergence of two moving averages of different duration as described above may be a "buy signal" and the beginning of their subsequent convergence may constitute a "sell signal."

More generally, comparing trailing moving averages of different periods is a useful tool for analyzing time series of data. As shown by Figure 3.2, it is very easy to detect the places at which moving averages with different trailing periods either diverge or converge. Analog displays of the data themselves can show upward or downward trends in the recorded values of the data. However, comparing moving averages of different trailing periods can quickly and unambiguously show whether such upward or downward trends are accelerating at a particular time. Furthermore, these relative rates of change can be quantified. The eye can estimate and the computer can easily calculate the angles between moving averages with different trailing periods. The greater the angle of the divergence of the two moving averages, the greater is the rate of that divergence. Such angles of divergence, whether expressed in degrees, radians or as trigonometric functions, such as the cosines of the angles between the diverging moving averages, can themselves be used as quantitative criteria for analyzing the data.

ADDITIONAL TYPES OF MOVING AVERAGES

Traditionally, the moving averages used to smooth data are trailing moving averages as described above. These are especially appropriate when the moving averages are used to help predict future phenomena like the change in the price of a stock. However, there are many other applications of moving averages that do not require them to be calculated in real time. Instead, the moving averages can be calculated retrospectively by using data that have been recorded and then stored, even for a brief period. For example, one might have a database consisting of sequentially recorded and stored computerized data and for which one wanted to calculate 10-sample moving averages. Besides calculating 10-sample *trailing* moving averages, one can also calculate the 10-sample *central* moving average (CMA). For the former, one uses the 10 preceding data points to compute the average. For the latter, one uses the five preceding and the five succeeding data points to calculate the average. For example, for position #11 in the series of data, the 10-sample trailing moving average would be the arithmetic mean of data point one through data point 10. For position #11 in the same series, the 10-sample CMA would be the arithmetic mean of data point 6 through data point 10 plus data point 12 through data point 16. An advantage of the CMA is that by using both preceding and subsequent data points, it more accurately reflects the actual position of the moving average in the series of data, rather than the position of only the data points that preceded it.

It is also possible that other metrics are superior to the arithmetic mean for accurately identifying meaningful clusters in time series of data. There is not *a priori* way to determine either the optimal smoothing parameter or the best sample size to use for calculating that parameter. Therefore, these questions must be answered empirically, and the following section of this chapter describes evidence that has been gathered for this purpose.

COMPARING PARAMETERS FOR DETECTING CLUSTERED EVENTS

Since there are a number of possible methods for smoothing data, a study was conducted to compare the methods with respect to their abilities to detect events of interest. The study tested the ability of the recorded values of a computerized digital ECG parameter to detect a particular type of heart attack – prior inferior myocardial infarction (MI). The index parameter is the duration of Q waves in milliseconds. In ECG lead aVF, the smoothing parameters are derivatives of lead aVF Q-wave duration. A Q wave is an early downward deflection in the part of a standard ECG tracing that represents the electrical activation of the main pumping chambers of the heart. Lead aVF is one of the 12 standard ECG leads. The duration of Q waves in ECG lead aVF is a widely used parameter for diagnosing prior inferior MI, because patients with inferior MI tend to have more prolonged (measured in milliseconds) Q waves in lead aVF than do patients without prior inferior MI [5,6]. Prior posterior myocardial MI, although less prevalent than prior inferior MI, is also associated with abnormally prolonged Q waves in lead aVF [7–10].

To compare the different methods of smoothing data, the study used a simulated time series of data using ECG measurements obtained from a group of patients who had been evaluated for possible coronary artery disease using criteria that are entirely independent of the ECG. In this simulation, each column of data contains the computerized measurements of various ECG parameters, and each row contains the specific values of these measurements exhibited by each patient. In a time series, each sequential change in the value of a parameter represents a change from one time interval to the next. In the present simulated time series, each sequentially recorded value of the parameter represents a change from one patient to the next. Thus, changes in the parameters' values over a series of different patients are surrogates for changes in those values in the same patient over a period of time, e.g., as would occur during the medical monitoring of a patient. In this simulated time series, the relevant diagnosis of each patient was independently corroborated by either cardiac catheterization (67%) or by systematic clinical evaluation using screening criteria exclusive of the ECG (33%).

The study used ECG data obtained from 2025 patients, each of whom had undergone cardiac catheterization. ($n = 1361$) or systematic clinical evaluation by two or more cardiologists ($n = 664$). Of the total, 366 had cath-proven prior inferior MI, and 497 patients had no significant coronary artery disease by catheterization. The other diagnostic categories in the database are prior posterior MI ($n = 66$), prior anterior MI ($n = 275$), combined prior inferior and anterior MI ($n = 157$) and screening normal ($n = 664$). As is customary in the evaluation of diagnostic criteria, the database is sequentially divided into a learning set and a test set of approximately equal size. In the learning set and in the test set, respectively, the ECG data were sequentially clustered with respect to each of the above six angiographic and clinical screening categories.

The study compared the diagnostic performances of the raw lead aVF Q-wave duration data, and the following methods of smoothing the recorded lead aVF Q-wave duration data:

1. The 10-sample CMA of the lead aVF Q-wave duration data – consisting the mean of the five Q-wave duration measurements immediately preceding it, plus the five Q-wave duration measurements immediately following it. In addition to the 10-sample CMAs, CMA that used eight, six, four, and two samples were evaluated.
2. The 10-sample central moving median – the median of the five Q-wave duration measurements immediately preceding it, plus the five Q-wave duration measurements immediately following it.
3. The 10-sample central moving mode – the mode of the five Q-wave duration measurements immediately preceding it, plus the five Q-wave duration measurements immediately following it. The

mode of a group of numerical values is the value that occurs most frequently.

4. The 10-sample central moving maximum – the maximum value of the five Q-wave duration measurements immediately preceding it, plus the five Q-wave duration measurements immediately following it.
5. The 10-sample central moving minimum – the minimum value of the five Q-wave duration measurements immediately preceding it, plus the five Q-wave duration measurements immediately following it.
6. The 10-sample central moving threshold count – this parameter consists of the number of Q-wave durations that were ≥ 30 ms in the five Q-wave duration measurements immediately preceding it, plus the five Q-wave duration measurements immediately following it. This threshold value was chosen because a Q-wave duration ≥ 30 ms in lead aVF is a widely used ECG diagnostic criterion for prior inferior MI [5,6].

The diagnostic sensitivity at 100% specificity of each of the above parameters was determined. Figures 3.3, 3.4, and 3.5 and Tables 3.1, 3.2, and 3.3 show the results of the study.

Figure 3.3 shows a line graph of the Q-wave durations in lead aVF when the data are grouped according to their diagnostic categories. The horizontal axis of the graph shows the diagnostic categories, and the vertical axis gives the Q-wave durations in milliseconds. The thin horizontal line shows the value of the data point above which the data

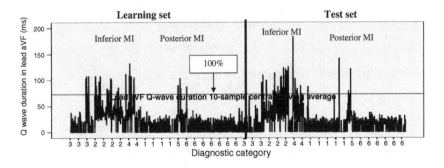

Fig. 3.3. ECG data clustered by diagnostic category lead aVF Q-wave duration raw data. A 10-s CMA, 10-sample central moving average; ECG, electrocardiographic; MI, myocardial infarction; ms, milliseconds; spec., specificity. Diagnostic categories: 1, normal by cardiac catheterization; 2, prior inferior MI; 3, prior anterior MI; 4, combined prior inferior and anterior MI; 5, prior posterior MI; 6, normal by clinical cardiological screening.

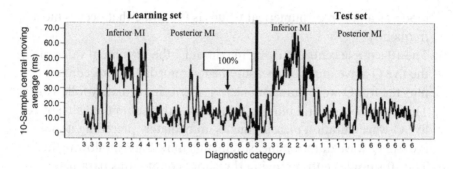

Fig. 3.4. ECG data clustered by diagnostic category lead aVF Q-wave 10-s CMA data. Refer to legend of Fig. 3.3.

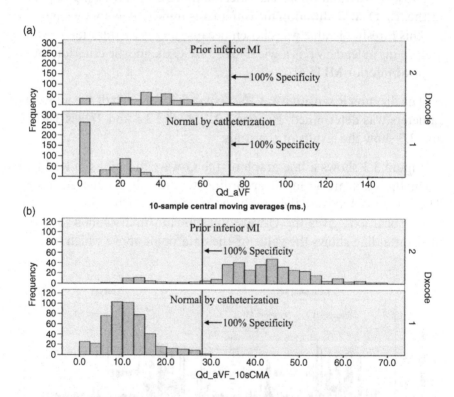

Fig. 3.5. Histograms of lead aVF Q-wave duration and 10-s CMA data in prior inferior MI versus normal subjects. (a) All data clustered by diagnostic category lead aVF Q-wave duration (ms). (b) A 10-sample central moving averages (ms). A 10-CMA, 10-sample central moving average; MI, myocardial infarction; ms, milliseconds; spec., specificity.

Table 3.1 Effects of the Type of Moving Average Data Clustered According to Diagnostic Category

Clustered Parameter	Threshold Value (ms)	% Sensitivity @100% Spec.	Chi Square*	Alpha*
aVF QD	73	11		
10-s CMA	28	90	456	4×10^{-101}
10-s median	31	86	414	5×10^{-92}
10-s mode	31	72	282	3×10^{-63}
10-s maximum	143	0	42	8×10^{-11}
10-s minimum	7	58	179	8×10^{-41}
10-s count ≥ 30	8.5	54	155	1×10^{-35}

CMA, central moving average; MI, myocardial infarction; ms, milliseconds; spec., specificity; 10-s CMA, central moving average (mean) of 10 value of 10 samples; 10-s mode, mode of 10 samples; ECG, electrocardiographic; NS, not significant; QD, Q-wave duration; spec., specificity samples; 10-s count ≥ 30, values ≥30 ms per 10 samples; 10-s maximum, largest value of 10 samples; 10-s median, median of 10 samples; 10-s minimum, smallest value of 10 samples.
* Compared to the parameter aVF QD.

Table 3.2 Effects of the Type of Moving Average Data *Not* Clustered According to Diagnostic Category

Nonclustered Parameter	Threshold Value (ms)	% Sensitivity @100% Spec.	Chi Square*	Alpha*
aVF QD	73	11		
10-s CMA	41	3	17.7	3×10^{-5}
10-s median	37	5	9.1	3×10^{-3}
10-s mode	51	0	42.3	8×10^{-11}
10-s maximum	163	1	31.3	2×10^{-8}
10-s minimum	6	3	17.7	3×10^{-5}
10-s count ≥ 30	8	3	17.7	3×10^{-5}

Refer to legend of Table 3.1.
* Compared to the parameter aVF QD.

Table 3.3 Effects of Sample Size in the Central Moving Average Data Clustered According to Diagnostic Category

Clustered Parameter	Threshold Value (ms)	% Sensitivity @100% Spec.	Chi Square*	P*
10-sample CMA	28	90		
8-sample CMA	30	88	0.68	NS
6-sample CMA	35	72	38	9×10^{-10}
4-sample CMA	45	38	214	2×10^{-48}
2-sample CMA	63	13	432	6×10^{-96}

Refer to legend for Table 3.1.
* Compared to the parameter 10-sample CMA.

exhibit 100% specificity for prior inferior MI. The thick vertical dotted line demarcates the learning set and the test set of data.

Figure 3.3 is a line graph of the stored raw QRS duration data. The learning set and the test set each show clusters of data labeled "inferior MI" and "posterior MI," in which the lead aVF Q-wave duration data tend to have higher values than those in the remainder of the graph. It is not surprising the "inferior MI" diagnostic cluster is much larger than "posterior MI" cluster because the former group contains 366 patients, and the latter group contains only 66 patients.

Figure 3.4 shows the 10-sample CMAs that were calculated using the same raw Q-wave duration data that are displayed in Figure 3.3. This graph of the moving averages shows clusters of similar size in the inferior and posterior MI groups in both the learning and the test sets. However, Figures 3.3 and 3.4 differ in several important respects. First the graph of the moving averages in Figure 3.4 is smoother, i.e., shows fewer sharp oscillations than the graph of the raw data in Figure 3.3. This greater smoothness of the moving average data makes the onsets and the offsets the clusters of the abnormal data especially easy to identify. Second, the graph of the moving averages in Figure 3.4 has a much greater proportion of values above the horizontal 100% specificity line than does the graph of the raw data in Figure 3.3. Third, the relative distances above the 100% specificity line are generally greater for the moving average data in Figure 3.4 than they are for the raw data in Figure 3.3. Fourth, examining the intersection of the horizontal 100% specificity line with the vertical axis shows that the value required to achieve 100% diagnostic specificity for prior inferior MI is much lower in the moving average data in Figure 3.4 than in the raw Q-wave duration data in Figure 3.3 (about 28 ms vs. about 70 ms).

The two histograms in the upper half of Figure 3.5 reveal that the raw QRS duration data discriminate poorly between the patients in the prior inferior MI versus the normal group. For example, most of the data points are on the left side of the vertical 100% specificity line in both the MI and normal groups. In contrast, the two histograms in the lower half of Figure 3.5 show that the 10-sample CMAs discriminate much more clearly between the prior MI versus the normal group. Unlike the raw data shown in the upper two histograms in Figure 3.5, the 10-sample CMAs in the lower two histograms reveal that most of the prior inferior MI 10-sample CMAs are to the right of the vertical 100% specificity line. In marked contrast to this, all the 10-sample CMA data for the normal group are to the left of the vertical 100% specificity line.

The histograms in Figure 3.5 reveal an additional important difference between the raw data and the CMAs. The histogram on the left side of the graph labeled "normal by catheterization" shows that the distribution of the raw Q-wave duration data is not Gaussian, i.e., bell-shaped. Instead, these data are heavily skewed to the right, with the most frequently recorded Q-wave duration being zero. This is because many people with normal hearts have no Q waves at all in lead aVF, and the value of Q-wave duration for such patients is therefore zero. However, on the lower half of Figure 3.4, the histogram labeled "normal by catheterization" shows that the distribution of the CMA data is Gaussian. This means the moving averages data permit the use of more robust parametric statistical methods for performing additional analyses the data. In contrast, in this particular case, one can use only less robust nonparametric statistical methods for further analyzing the data.

Tables 3.1, 3.2, and 3.3 provide additional information about the findings of this study. Each of these tables shows the abilities to detect inferior MI using lead aVF Q-wave duration data and various types of moving averages based on these data. In each table, the columns show from left to right:

1. The parameter being evaluated and whether it is being evaluated in a clustered or a nonclustered distribution.
2. The threshold value in milliseconds of each parameter that is needed to attain 100% diagnostic specificity.
3. The diagnostic sensitivity of each parameter at 100% specificity.
4. The chi square value calculated using a 2×2 matrix that compares the proportion of prior MI cases detected, using each type of moving average to the proportion of prior MI cases detected using the recorded raw lead aVF Q-wave duration data.
5. The statistical P values associated with each chi square value.

For example, the first row of data in Table 3.1 shows that the raw lead aVF Q-wave duration data require a value of 73 ms to yield 100%

specificity for prior inferior MI, and this value of 73 ms is associated with 11% diagnostic sensitivity. The second row of data in Table 3.1 reveals that the 10-s CMA requires only 28 ms to yield 100% specificity and is associated with a diagnostic sensitivity for prior inferior MI that is over eight times greater than that of the raw data. Not surprisingly, the last two columns in the same row show that this improvement in detecting prior MI that results from using the 10-sample moving average, rather than the raw data, is very highly statistically significant. The remaining rows of data in Table 3.1 show that the 10-sample median, mode, minimum, and threshold counts also have statistically significantly superior diagnostic performances compared to the raw data. Conversely, the performance of the 10-s maximum was significantly worse than that of the recorded raw data and failed to detect any cases at all at 100% specificity.

The format of Table 3.2 is identical to that of Table 3.1, but the results shown in it are substantially different. This is because of the differences in the way that the data were arranged. In Table 3.1, the data were clustered according the patients' diagnostic groups, i.e., normal, prior inferior MI, etc. In contrast, the results listed in Table 3.2 were obtained when the same patients were listed in order of their hospital identification numbers. These hospital numbers have nothing to do with their diagnoses. Therefore, the results shown in Table 3.1 were obtained when the data were clustered with respect to diagnosis, and those shown in Table 3.2 were obtained when they were not clustered according to diagnosis.

Table 3.2 shows that when the data are *not* clustered with respect to diagnosis, the performances associated with each type of moving average are statistically significantly worse than the performances based on the raw data. The contrast between the results shown using clustered data Table 3.1 versus nonclustered data Table 3.2 is not surprising. When the data are arranged with respect to diagnosis, any given data point that represents a patient with a particular diagnosis (prior inferior MI or a condition other than prior inferior MI) is nearly always associated with surrounding data points that are consistent with the same diagnosis. Since a given moving average reflects the influence of these surrounding data points, an abnormal value of the moving average in clustered data suggests that it is located within a cluster of similarly abnormal cases. In other words, the diagnostic meaning of a moving average is reinforced by the values of the data points around it. If the data are not clustered in this way, a given moving average reflects the influence of data points that could be either normal or abnormal in a completely random way. Therefore, a moving average that uses nonclustered data is likely to be less diagnostically useful than any single data point alone. In nonclustered data, the surrounding data points diminish, rather than reinforce, the importance of a given abnormal value.

As explained previously, actual time series of data that are relevant to detecting events of interest are clustered assuming that data are relevant to the event and that the frequency of sampling of the data is appropriate. This is because; except for the realm of quantum physics, events that occur in the world around us are extended in time. Therefore, the results shown in Table 3.1 are far more likely to be observed in actual time series than are the results shown in Table 3.2.

Table 3.3 reveals the effects of sample size in the use of CMAs. It shows that the 10-sample CMA exhibits 90% diagnostic sensitivity at 100% specificity. The eight-sample moving average has a slightly lower sensitivity, but the difference in diagnostic performance between it and the 10-sample average is not statistically significant. Table 3.3 also shows that as diagnostic sensitivity decreases, the threshold value required to attain 100% specificity increases.

CALCULATING MOVING AVERAGES ON THE PERSONAL COMPUTER

The mathematical and graphical capabilities of widely used commercial software make it extremely easy to calculate and display CMA when analyzing time series of data. For example, the following are the steps for calculating the 10-sample CMAs using the spreadsheet program Microsoft Excel:

1. Arrange the recorded raw values of the data points sequentially in a column (e.g., Column A) so that the earliest value in the time series is at the top of the column (e.g., Row 1) and the next value is immediately below it.
2. Use the adjacent column (Column B) to calculate and display the CMAs of the recorded raw data as follows.

3. Beginning at Column B, Row 6 enter the formula:

$$= \text{Average}(A1 : A5, A7:A11)$$

4. This formula will calculate the arithmetic mean of the 10 raw data points recorded in Column A Rows 1 through 5, plus those in Column A, Rows 6 through 10.
5. Copy this command to all the remaining cells in Column B that are adjacent to recorded values of raw data.
6. Column B will now contain the 10-sample CMAs of all the recorded raw data in Column A.
7. Use the graphical capabilities of Excel to generate a line or column graph of the moving averages and, if desired, the recorded raw data as well. If the line graph option is chosen, the resulting graph should generally resemble those shown in Figures 3.3 and 3.4.

Current versions of commercial spreadsheet programs can accommodate enormous amounts of data. For example, each column of Excel can accommodate more than 16,000 columns and over one million rows of data. Needless to say, the availability of 16 billion cells for data entry makes it possible to handle very long time series.

THE IMPORTANCE OF CLUSTERED DATA AND MOVING AVERAGES

Clustered data are extremely abundant. This is because all the events we experience and that we might wish to identify, understand, and act upon have finite and measurable durations. It therefore follows that the individual data points associated with each instance of such an event are clustered with respect to time. Many events associated with clustered data, such as medical and seismic phenomena, can be highly significant, and it is therefore important to identify them as accurately as possible. The findings described in this chapter show that the use of CMAs greatly improves the ease and accuracy with which one can identify clusters of evidence for events of interest. The "smoothing" of data that the moving averages produce does far more than merely improve the appearance of analog depictions of data. The moving averages also dramatically increase the accuracy with which one can identify and characterize the events that the data were collected to reveal.

Although a variety of statistical measures and sample sizes can be used to calculate moving average, the present study shows that the 10-s CMA produced the best results.

The rationale for the use of the CMA is compelling. The CMA incorporates the data from multiple proximate instances of the same abnormality in each cluster. In other words, in data relevant to clustered events of interest, the likelihood that each data point is a true positive or a true negative increases if it is surrounded by other data with similar values. The diagnostic categorization of each data point is reinforced by those of its neighbors. The phenomenon of being surrounded by other data obviously confers a diagnostic advantage only if the data are clustered with respect to the same diagnosis. The data used in the present study represent a simulated, rather than a true, time series. However, whether each datum represents a different patient instead of a different point in time, the data will still be clustered with respect to a phenomenon of interest.

The present study has emphasized the use of 10 samples for calculating the CMAs. However, as shown by the findings listed in Table 3.3, using eight samples for calculating the CMAs produced a statistically similar diagnostic result. Table 3.3 also shows that as the number of samples used to calculate the CMA decreases, the diagnostic threshold needed to reach 100% specificity increases. The data in Table 3.3 show that this increase in the threshold values required for 100% diagnostic specificity is non-linear. At CMA sample sizes less than six, diagnostic sensitivities at 100% specificity diminish rapidly.

Comparing Figure 3.3 to Figure 3.4 confirms that plotting the 10-s CMA data produces a smoother graph than plotting the raw lead aVF Q-wave data. The greater smoothness of the graph in Figure 3.4 is evident, despite the fact that it incorporates nearly as many data points as the graph in Figure 3.3 (2020 vs. 2025). The greater smoothness of the line graph in Figure 3.4 occurs because the process of averaging the raw data to produce each value of the CMA attenuates the effect of the data point to data point variation in the raw data. The greater smoothness of the CMA graph compared to the raw data graph is of more than aesthetic importance. It may improve the accuracy with which one can review time series of data by making it easier to identify the onsets and offsets of events of interest.

Nevertheless, it remains important to analyze the data numerically. This is because artifacts are often clustered as well. For example, in the medical monitoring of patients with possible cardiac disease, changes in the ECG can occur not only because of arrhythmias or episodes of myocardial ischemia, but also if the patient moves in bed or if one or more of the ECGs leads becomes loose. Therefore, it is important to determine the diagnostic thresholds of the clusters associated with myocardial ischemia so that they can be distinguished from artifacts with qualitatively similar appearances. Also, in seismography, it is important to know the thresholds needed to detect foreshock swarms of seismic activity and distinguish them from vibrations produced by intermittent highway or railway traffic.

The use of moving averages is important because most events that are of interest to us are not instantaneous, but instead are extended in time. Therefore, data that can be used identify and quantify these events occur in temporal clusters. Moving average parameters such as the 10-s CMA not only produce appealing visual depictions of the events, but also can also significantly improve our ability to identify and understand them.

REFERENCES

[1] Chatfield C. The analysis of time series, an introduction. 6th ed New York: Chapman & Hall/ CRC; 2004.

[2] Karl JH. An introduction to digital signal processing. San Diego, CA: Academic Press, Inc; 1989. 92101.

[3] Lyons RG. Understanding digital signal processing. Upper Saddle River: Prentice Hall PTR; 2001.

[4] Penzias AA, Wilson RW. A measurement of the flux density of CAS a at 4080 Mc/s. Astrophys J Lett 1965;142:1149–54.

[5] Warner RA, Wagner GS, Ideker RE. The ability of the QRS complex to determine the location and size of myocardial infarcts in Acute Coronary Care. Boston: Martinus Nijhoff; 1984.

[6] Warner RA, Hill N, Sheehe P, Mookherjee S, Fruehan. Improved criteria for the diagnosis of inferior myocardial infarction. Circulation 1982;66:422–8.

[7] Warner R. New developments in quantitative electrocardiography. Proc Eng Found 1986;10:207–1207.

[8] Hill NE, Warner RA, Mookherjee S, Smulyan H. Comparison of optimal scalar electrocardiographic, orthogonal electrocardiographic and vectorcardiographic criteria for diagnosing inferior and anterior myocardial infarction. Am J Cardiol 1984;54:274–6.

[9] Warner RA, Battaglia J, Hill NE, Mookherjee S, Smulyan H. Importance of the terminal por-
     tion of the QRS in the electrocardiographic diagnosis of inferior myocardial infarction. Am J
     Cardiol 1985;55:896–9.

[10] Warner RA, Hill NE, Mookherjee S, Smulyan H. Electrocardiographic criteria for the diag-
     nosis of combined inferior myocardial infarction and left anterior hemiblock. Am J Cardiol
     1983;51:718–22.

CHAPTER 4

Using Composite Analog Displays to Summarize and Interpret Data

A basic purpose of collecting and analyzing data is to acquire as much accurate and useful information as the data are able to provide. The subjects of our reviews of data may be specific things that are of particular interest to us. Alternatively, our reasons for gathering and evaluating data may be much broader in scope and include learning about various types of events and phenomena to gain a more complete understanding of them. In this regard, the field of statistics involves selecting and using methods for inferring justifiable general conclusions from the analysis of specific samples of data. Even more broadly, the method of inquiry used by all the branches of science is induction – the process of examining specific bits of evidence to generate and test hypotheses. If corroborated, these hypotheses may then lead us to a broader and deeper understanding of the world in which we live.

As has been emphasized, the values of individual members of a set of data frequently show substantial variability. This is often the case, even when these individuals share a common classification. For example, a large number of living beings on our planet can be correctly classified as "human male." However, the members of that general category vary widely with respect to many characteristics, e.g., age, height, weight, skin color, amount of facial hair, etc. In fact, the meaningful classification of living things can be so complex that an important branch of both zoology and botany is taxonomy – the classification of animals and plants based on their anatomical, physiological, and biochemical characteristics. Even in the process of scientific classification, we must answer the basic questions, "Where do we lump?" versus "Where do we split?" By what specific criteria do we decide whether two or more relatively similar things should belong to the same or to different groups? In other words, given the heterogeneity of individual examples of the various things we observe, how can we determine the features that permit us to classify them in the most reliable and useful ways? Answering these questions is necessary if we wish to develop the best rules for identifying most of the individual instances of them. The following are examples of contexts in which such questions arise:

- Developing the best set of rules for detecting specific diseases is the basic task of medical diagnostics. Knowing that different diseases have overlapping manifestations (e.g., fever, abnormalities of certain laboratory tests), how does one determine that a particular disease is present so that one can provide the most appropriate treatment for it?
- Geologists recognize that episodes of increased of seismic activity called "foreshock swarms" typically precede major earthquakes. On the other hand, many episodes of seismic activity that resemble foreshock swarms are *not* followed by earthquakes. Therefore, given the enormous amount of data that seismographs all over the world provide, can we develop reliable rules for identifying the mild episodes of seismic activity that are most likely to be harbingers of destructive earthquakes in the near future?
- Meteorologists have access to extremely large amounts of data concerning barometric pressure, wind direction and velocity, and atmospheric and oceanic temperatures. How can they use these data to develop the best rules for accurately predicting the locations, severity, and timing of destructive storms?
- Engineers may observe certain changes in an electronic or mechanical device in the course of its operation. What are the characteristics of such changes that are associated with impending failure of the device versus those that are merely minor aberrations in its performance?

The problem of determining the most generally recognizable characteristics of a particular phenomenon is especially great when one is dealing with analog data such as seismograms and ECG tracings. This is because with digital data, one can apply to the analysis well-established descriptors of central tendency (such as arithmetic mean, mode, and median) and of dispersion (such as standard deviation (SD), confidence intervals, and interquartile range). When dealing with analog data, however, one faces the much greater challenge of producing some sort of "visual average" to represent the data in a meaningful way. Such a general visual depiction of the analog data that are associated with a particular condition of interest can be very useful. It can demonstrate the features of individual analog displays that are most likely to be associated with that condition of interest. Such visual averages of analog displays could reveal commonalities among different instances of the same phenomenon that would otherwise be inapparent.

It is particularly important to optimize analog depictions of data because the human eye and brain are so adept at recognizing even complex visual patterns [1–3]. Nevertheless, in trying to identify particular conditions of interest using pattern recognition, we must address the problem of the heterogeneity exhibited by the individual examples of those conditions. We must distinguish between patterns that are merely atypical instances of the conditions of interest from those that do not represent these conditions at all [4]. The composite analog display is a tool for doing this. This chapter describes the method for producing and using them.

Besides helping to identify individual cases of various conditions of interest, analog displays can also improve our understanding of the mechanisms of many phenomena. For example, the study of analog recordings of the heart's electrical activity greatly helped to elucidate the mechanisms responsible for both lethal and non-lethal cardiac arrhythmias. This raises the question of which general type of analog pattern most reliably reflects the nature of the condition being investigated. Since a single instance of a phenomenon that we are trying to understand may be atypical in one or more ways, it is much more reliable to consider an analog display that represents a wide range of the possible specific manifestations of that phenomenon.

Using widely available and familiar commercial software, the author has developed and tested methods for optimizing the ability of analog displays of data to identify conditions of interest [4–7]. The methods account for the variability of the patterns that individual cases of the conditions frequently exhibit. One of the methods accomplishes this by producing visual averages of separate sets of analog data. One set of analog data is associated with the condition that one wishes to detect. The remaining, or "comparison set," of data is associated with the absence of that condition.

The specific task to which these methods were applied was that of determining what specific pattern of analog data should be for diagnosing an important type of heart attack – inferior myocardial infarction (MI). The analog representation of the data is the standard ECG tracing. More specifically, it was the QRS complex of the ECG tracing in standard lead aVF [8–10]. The QRS complex is that portion of the ECG tracing that depicts the voltages generated by the heart's ventricles during the process of electrical depolarization of the heart's ventricles. Lead aVF is one of the twelve standard ECG leads that is used to record the heart's electrical activity during the various phases of the cardiac cycle.

In recording the electrical activity of the heart, modern ECG machines record and store the data in digital form. The individual data points recorded by the ECG machine represent the potential differences (in microvolts) generated by the heart tissue at each interval of sampling (in the present case, every 4 ms). The graphics module that is part of the ECG machine's computer then uses these digital data to generate line graphs that constitute the familiar ECG waveforms. Thus, the standard ECG is an analog depiction of the heart's electrical activity. Just as the familiar analog representation of the ECG can be studied to identify various types of heart disease, the digital data that were used to produce this analog display can also be used to augment one's diagnostic efforts.

To develop and test the method of using visual averages of data, I studied the QRS complexes in standard lead aVF of the electrocardiograms of 862 patients who had undergone cardiac catheterization. Of these patients, the normal group consists of 497 (58%) with no evidence of coronary artery disease by cardiac catheterization. The inferior MI group consists of the remaining 365 patients with evidence of prior inferior MI by cardiac catheterization. The digital ECG QRS data from each of the 862 patients was then downloaded from the ECG machines to a Microsoft Excel® spreadsheet for analysis.

Figures 4.1 and 4.2 demonstrate the heterogeneity that individual QRS complexes exhibit, even though they have similar diagnostic classifications. Figure 4.1 shows wide variability among the analog displays of four different individual normal patients. Figure 4.2 shows similar variability in the shapes of the QRS complex among four patients with inferior MI. By comparing the group of examples from normal patients

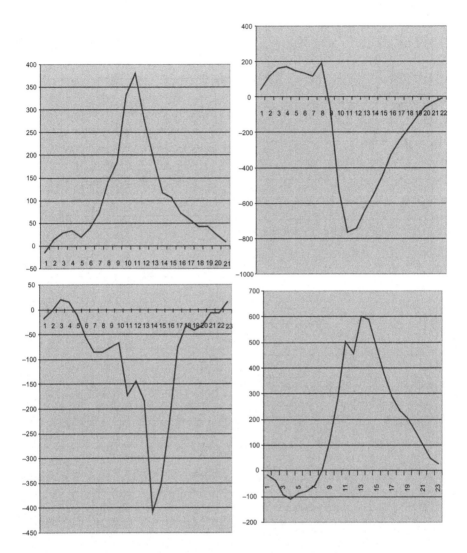

Fig. 4.1. QRS complexes in lead aVF examples of individual tracings in the normal group.

with the group of examples from the patients with inferior MI, it would be very difficult to generalize reliable rules for distinguishing between the normal and the inferior MI groups.

To devise a method of distinguishing reliably between patients in the normal group versus those in the inferior MI group, it is necessary to understand exactly how the digital data are arrayed in the Excel spreadsheet.

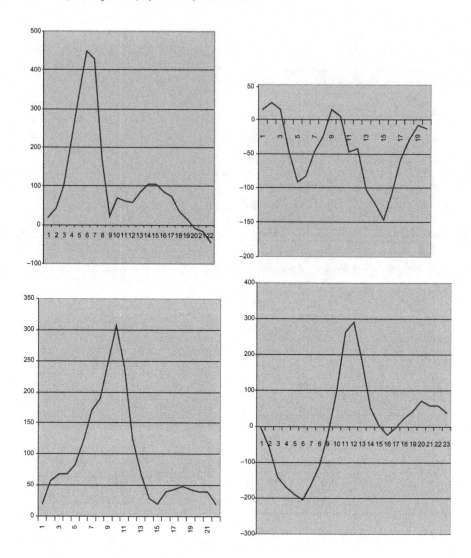

Fig. 4.2. QRS complexes in lead aVF examples of individual tracings in the inferior MI group.

Table 4.1 shows how the digital ECG QRS data are arranged in the spreadsheet. The top row shows the number of the sampling interval that is represented by the data in that column. For example, under the heading "20 ms" are all the data that were recorded at the 20-ms sampling interval, i.e., 20 ms after the onset of the QRS complex. In this illustration, the data that are represented are from the 4-ms samples through the 48-ms sample. Each "#" symbol represents a voltage measurement

Table 4.1 Digital ECG Data Spreadsheet Array

Patient No.	4 ms	8 ms	12 ms	16 ms	20 ms	24 ms	28 ms	32 ms	36 ms	40 ms	44 ms	48 ms
1	#	#	#	#	#	#	#	#	#	#	#	#
2	#	#	#	#	#	#	#	#	#	#	#	#
3	#	#	#	#	#	#	#	#	#	#	#	#
4	#	#	#	#	#	#	#	#	#	#	#	#
5	#	#	#	#	#	#	#	#	#	#	#	#
6	#	#	#	#	#	#	#	#	#	#	#	#
Mean												

in microvolts, and each row represents the recorded voltages for a separate patient. To produce an analog ECG QRS display for Patient 1, one would designate in the spreadsheet the numbers given in the first row and then use the graphics function of the spreadsheet to produce a line graph of those data. The actual array in the spreadsheet includes the ECG QRS data in lead aVF of all 497 normal patients and all 365 patients with inferior MI. To produce a "visual average" display for all the normal patients, one then uses the calculation function of the spreadsheet to calculate the arithmetic means of the voltage data in each column. In the example shown in Table 1.1, the last row of the table contains these calculated mean voltages. Generating a line graph of the mean voltages would then produce a line graph that represents a visual average analog display of the ECG QRS data in lead aVF of all 497 normal patients. By following similar steps for the ECG data recorded from inferior MI patients, one can generate a separate visual average of the QRS ECG data from all 365 of these patients as well.

Since the averages of the voltages in the normal group incorporate the voltages of all 497 normal patients, they constitute a composite of 497 data points at each interval of sampling. Therefore, a graph of these averages is a composite analog display of the ECG QRS data from the normal group. Similarly, a graph of the average voltages at each sampling interval in the inferior MI group is a composite analog display of the inferior MI ECG QRS data. By comparing these composite analog displays from each group, it is possible to determine the ways in which normal group patients and patients with inferior MI are most likely to differ with respect to their ECG QRS complexes in lead aVF.

   The composite graphs of the normal patients and of the inferior
MI patients are shown in Figure 4.3. The *X*- and *Y*-axes are the same
as those in Figures 4.1 and 4.2. The vertical axis shows the amplitude
of the QRS voltages in microvolts, and each individual point on the
X-axis represents the recorded voltage at each 4.0 ms sampling interval.
Comparison of the individual ECG QRS displays shown in Figures 4.1
and 4.2 had revealed no obvious differences between the normal and the
inferior MI groups. In contrast, the composite analog displays shown in
Figure 4.3 discriminate very clearly between the normal and the inferior
MI groups. In Figure 4.3, the composite display of the normal group
and of the inferior MI group are superimposed upon one another. It

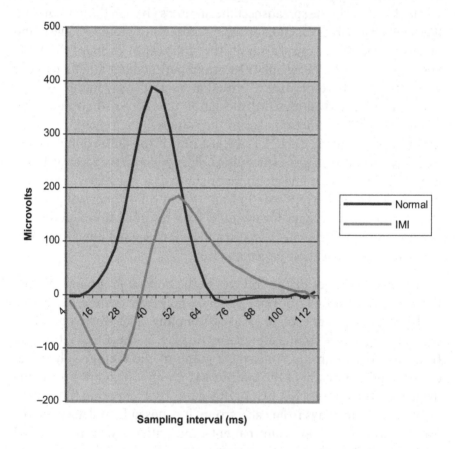

Fig. 4.3. Composite analog displays lead aVF QRS morphology in normal versus IMI groups mean voltages at each sampling interval.

shows that the composite ECG QRS display of the normal group (in black) is almost entirely above the X-axis. This means that the voltages recorded at nearly all the sampling intervals have positive values. In marked contrast, the composite ECG QRS display of the inferior MI group (in gray) begins with a deep and prolonged deflection below the X-axis. This means that the voltages recorded during the initial part of the ECG QRS complex have negative values. This initial negative deflection occurred in the 4th through the 32nd sampling intervals of the QRS. Furthermore, Figure 4.3 shows that when the composite graph of the inferior MI data eventually becomes positive, its maximum amplitude is much lower than the maximum amplitude of the positive deflection of the normal patients' composite graph.

Perhaps the most important observation to make at this point is that Figure 4.3 illustrates the great instructional value that composite graphs can have. Even if one had no previous training or experience in interpreting ECGs, examining the composite graphs in Figure 4.3 clearly reveals the following: compared to normal individuals, patients with inferior MI tend to have prominently negative initial deflections of the ECG QRS complex in lead aVF. Such an observation is far from trivial. If one had the task of developing precise quantitative diagnostic ECG criteria for inferior MI, the composite analog displays shown in Figure 4.3 strongly and correctly suggest that the initial portion of the QRS complex in lead aVF is an excellent place on which to focus one's efforts [8–10].

Electrocardiography is by no means the only field in which composite analog displays can be useful. For example, it is known that destructive earthquakes are often preceded by mild increases in seismic activity called "foreshock swarms." These are episodes in which seismographs record increases in the amplitude and frequency of seismic activity. However, similar mild increases in seismic activity often occur without being followed by earthquakes [11]. Perhaps composite analog displays of seismographic data can be used to improve the accuracy with which earthquakes can be predicted. To do so, one could use previously recorded episodes of mild increases in seismic activity for two separate groups. One group would be those episodes of mildly increased seismic activity that had been followed by earthquakes. The other group would be those episodes of mildly increased seismic activity that had *not* been followed by them. Using techniques similar to those described for ECG, a composite analog display could be made of the recorded seismographic data for the "earthquake group" and a separate one for the "non-earthquake group." By comparing these two composite analog displays, it may be possible to optimize the predictive utility of seismographic data. Such a study would be entirely feasible, since like contemporary ECG machines, modern seismographic equipment records and stores seismic data in digital form and then graphs those data to produce the familiar analog seismogram.

A similar approach might be used for any type of recorded data that might be relevant to the occurrence of events of interest in a large number of different fields. The described method can even be used with data that has been stored by various devices in analog form. Electronic digitizers can be used on analog tracings to convert the data to the necessary numerical form.

The application of composite analog displays can be further refined. This refinement involves the use of Z scores that were discussed in detail in Chapter 2. For example, with arrays of data similar to the one shown in Table 1.1, the spreadsheet can easily calculate the mean, SD, and Z scores of the data. Returning to the previously discussed study, one could use the spreadsheet to quickly calculate the mean and SD of the ECG QRS data at each 4-ms sampling interval for the group of 497 normal patients. One can then use the results of these calculations to have the spreadsheet rapidly calculate the Z scores of each of the 365 inferior MI patients for each sampling interval using this formula:

$$Z \text{ score} = \frac{\text{Data point from inferior MI group} - \text{Mean of normal group}}{\text{SD of normal group}}$$

Next, one can calculate the averages of the inferior MI Z scores for each of the intervals of sampling. Plotting a line graph of these Z scores produces a composite analog Z score display for the inferior MI patients as shown in Figure 4.4.

Not surprisingly, the composite analog Z score display of the inferior MI group in Figure 4.4 has a contour similar to that of the composite analog voltage display of the inferior MI group shown in Figure 4.3. Both of the composite analog displays are characterized by prolonged

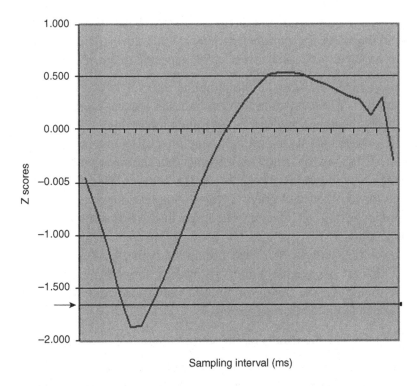

Fig. 4.4. Z scores of the inferior MI group composite analog display ECG QRS complex in lead aVF.

downward initial deflections (meaning that both the voltages and the Z scores are negative) followed by a relatively low amplitude upward deflection. However, the horizontal line marked by the arrow near the bottom of the line graph in Figure 4.4 shows that the composite Z score display has an advantage over the composite display of the voltages. This horizontal line designates a Z score of -1.65. As explained in Chapter 2 about Z scores, any Z score below this value is statistically significantly lower than the corresponding value of the normal group at $P < 0.05$. For the data displayed in Figure 4.4, only the inferior MI Z scores of the 20th, 24th, and 28th ms sampling intervals attained this level of statistical significance.

This observation suggests that to develop especially reliable criteria for inferior MI using ECG QRS data in lead aVF, using the data from the 20th, 24th, and 28th intervals of sampling is likely to be especially effective.

To evaluate the importance of these observations, the diagnostic abilities of the following parameters were compared by determining their respective diagnostic sensitivities at 98% specificity for inferior MI:

1. The voltage data from all the sampling intervals of the QRS complex – These are data that can be used with *no composites* to suggest the use of any specific sampling intervals.
2. The voltage data from only sampling intervals 4 ms through 32 ms – These are the sampling intervals that the *analog voltage composites* showed to discriminate best between the normal and inferior MI groups. At each of these sampling intervals, the normal composite and the inferior MI composite have directionally opposite deflections.
3. The voltage data from only sampling intervals 20, 24, and 28 ms – These are the sampling intervals of the inferior MI group that the analog *Z score composite* showed were statistically significantly different from the normal group.

Table 4.2 lists the results of this comparison.

Table 4.2 shows that using either the composite voltage analog display or the composite Z score analog display results in a highly significant improvement in diagnostic sensitivity for inferior MI, compared to using the voltage data at all the sampling intervals. Furthermore, using the Z score composite display results in a further significant improvement in diagnostic performance compared to using the voltage composite.

These findings are consistent with important principles of data analysis. First, they illustrate the point that when examining and analyzing

Table 4.2 Diagnostic Performances for Detecting Inferior MI

Parameters	Sens. (%)	Spec. (%)	Chi Sq.	P Value
All samples	5	98		
Samples 4–32 (voltage composites)	34	98	98*	4×10^{-23}*
Samples 20–28 (Z score composite)	52	98	199* 24**	4×10^{-45}* 8×10^{-7}**

Chi sq., chi square analysis; sens., sensitivity; spec., specificity.
* Compared to all samples.
** Compared to voltage composites.

data, it is important to know upon which portions and which features of the data to concentrate. Using the analog voltage composite to determine the choice of which specific sampling intervals to use for diagnostic purposes resulted in nearly a sevenfold increase in sensitivity at the same high specificity.

Second, using the analog Z score composite produced a diagnostic performance that was even better than that exhibited by the voltage composite. Why should this be the case? The answer is that whereas the voltage composite employs only the parameter of the mean voltage at each sampling interval, the Z score composite uses both the parameters of the mean voltage and the SD of the voltage at each sampling interval. The SD is a measure of the observed variation in a set of data. Therefore, when a data point has an abnormal Z score, it means not only that the data point is higher or lower than the mean value of a comparison population, but also that the magnitude of this difference exceeds what would be expected from the amount of random variation of the data's values in the comparison population. In other words, the difference is greater than one would expect to have occurred by chance alone.

The analysis of analog patterns is important for identifying and understanding conditions of interest in such diverse fields as engineering, medicine, statistics, economics, and the social and physical sciences. Therefore, composite analog displays can play an important role. By helping to teach us which portions of an analog display contain the most useful information, they can help us take full advantage of our great ability to recognize visual patterns [1–3]. Using an example that is relevant to the data presented in this chapter, a cardiologist might be presented with arrays of digital data that can be used to generate a standard analog ECG waveform. However, it is likely that he will be able to interpret the analog waveform more efficiently than would be possible by examining only the digital data. This is largely because the human brain is so highly adept at recognizing visual patterns.

In studying analog displays of data, however, the reviewer must have reliable answers to these questions:

1. What types of patterns in the displays should I be looking for?

2. How much deviation from an expected pattern should be considered abnormal?
3. Which, if any, portions of the analog display meet that criterion for abnormality?

Together, the composite raw data and the composite Z score analog displays provide answers to all three of these questions.

REFERENCES

[1] Milewski R, Govindaraju V. Binarization and cleanup of handwritten text and carbon copy medical form images. Pattern Recog 2008;41(4):1308–15.

[2] Nelson CA. The development and neural bases of face recognition. Infant Child Dev 2001;10(1–2):3–18.

[3] Duda RO, Hart PE, Stork DG. Pattern classification. 2nd ed New York: Wiley; 2001.

[4] Warner RA, Olicker AL, Haisty WK, Hill NE, Selvester RH, Wagner GS. The importance of accounting for the variability of electrocardiographic data among diagnostically similar patients. Am J Cardiol 2000;86:1238–40.

[5] Warner RA. Using standardized numerical scores for the display and interpretation of biomedical data. In: Arabnia HR, Tran Q, editors. Adv Exp Med Biol (Software Tools and Algorithms for Biological Systems). New York: Springer; 2010. p. 725–31.

[6] Warner RA. Color-coded z scores for the display and analysis of biomedical data. 2nd World Congress on Biomarkers and Clinical Research. J Mol Biomark Diagn 2011;2(4):33.

[7] Warner RA. Using composite digital data to improve the interpretation of analog displays. In: Arabnia HR, Tran Q, Yang M, editors. Proceedings of the 2014 International Conference on Bioinformatics and Computational Biology. USA: CSREA Press; 2014. p. 188–93.

[8] Warner RA, Hill NE, Mookherjee S, Smulyan H. Improved electrocardiographic criteria for the diagnosis of left anterior hemiblock. Am J Cardiol 1983;51:723–6.

[9] Warner RA, Hill NE, Sheehe PR, Mookherjee S, Fruehan CT, Smulyan H. Improved electrocardiographic criteria for the diagnosis of inferior myocardial infarction. Circulation 1982;66:422–8.

[10] Warner RA, Hill NE. Optimized electrocardiographic criteria for prior inferior and an anterior myocardial infarction. J Electrocardiol 2012;45:209–13.

[11] McGuire JJ, Boettcher MS, Jordan TH. Foreshock sequences and short-term earthquake predictability on East Pacific Rise transform faults. Nature 2005;434(7032):457–61.

CHAPTER 5

The Stacked Frame Display for the Rapid Review and Analysis of Data

In medicine and in many other fields such as seismology and engineering, it is often important to examine large amounts of data to detect important patterns in the information. These data frequently represent time series in which the data points are acquired sequentially over a given period. For example, many patients with known or suspected heart disease undergo ambulatory electrocardiographic (ECG) monitoring to detect, characterize, and quantify episodes of various abnormalities whose presence may put the patient at increased risk for disability or death. It is widely accepted that ambulatory ECG monitoring, which may last for hours or days, is a useful clinical tool [1–6]. This is because physicians are often interested in whether patients are getting these abnormalities in the course of their customary daily lives rather than in a much less typical hospital setting. However, studies have shown that current methods of detecting both arrhythmias and ischemia using the ambulatory ECG are suboptimal [4–6]. Improvements in electromagnetic and optical storage have permitted the collection of large amounts of clinically important data generated by ambulatory monitoring. This has made the use of accurate and efficient methods for reviewing these data especially important. For example, consider a 3-day recording of data recorded by three standard ECG leads from a patient whose average heart rate is 70 beats/min. The number of individual ECG complexes to be reviewed is:

$$3\,\text{leads} \times 70\,\text{beats/min} \times 60\,\text{min/h} \times 24\,\text{h/day} \times 3\,\text{days}$$
$$= 907,200\,\text{ECG complexes}$$

Furthermore, each ECG complex has multiple components, any combination of which may exhibit transient or persistent abnormalities in amplitude and/or duration. The considerable time required to review recordings such as these not only makes the process inefficient and therefore costly, but can also compromise the accuracy of the interpretations. First, the tedium associated with examining very large amounts of data can lead to intermittent inattention to the task at hand. Second, because of the large amounts of time required, it is often decided that it is not feasible for a physician expert in electrocardiography to review all the ECG complexes that have been recorded during hours or days of monitoring. Therefore, it is common practice to have less highly trained technicians review the data first and then select portions of the original recording for subsequent review by a physician. Therefore, if a technician happens to miss important recorded events because of either the tediousness of the task or a relative lack of expertise in electrocardiography, the physician never even gets to examine the important data. In other words, the current system of reviewing ambulatory ECG data does not provide "full disclosure" of the data to the experts who are the most qualified to interpret the information.

The present chapter describes a method of producing a meaningful display of even large amounts of sequentially acquired electronic data in a much smaller space than that which is required to display traditional analog tracings. The display is highly intuitive, and because of its compactness, it enables one to both review recorded data rapidly and to easily identify diagnostically useful patterns that otherwise would have been very difficult to detect. These features of the display eliminate the need for preliminary review of the data by a technician. Therefore, it provides full disclosure of the data to the individuals who have the greatest expertise in the interpretation of the information.

The method to be described and evaluated is called the stacked frame display (SFD) of analog data, and Figure 5.1 uses the P wave, QRS complex, and T wave of a typical ECG complex to demonstrate how the display is generated. First, as Figure 5.1 shows, the series of waves to be displayed is rotated 90°. This rotation causes the previously upright portions of the waves to point directly toward the observer and the previously downward portions of the waves to point directly away from the observer.

The 90° rotation reduces the height of all the parts of the original display to the width of a single line. Second, to restore the amplitude and duration information that had been given by the original analog display, one uses a system of coding that involves either different colors, shades of gray, or the relative brightness of a screen's pixels. For example, the portions of the waves that have rotated toward the observer could be

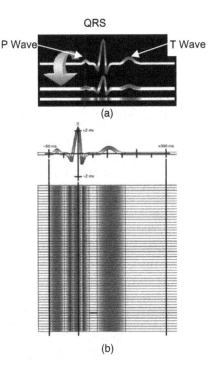

Fig. 5.1. Generation of the SFD.

colored red, and those that have rotated away from the observer could be colored blue. The intensities of each of these colors are proportional to the amplitudes of the waves being depicted. As also illustrated in Figure 5.1, information about the durations of each component of the original analog display is conveyed by the widths of the individual colored portions of each line.

In a sequential display of analog data, each set of rotated and encoded waves is placed either directly beneath or directly above its predecessor. In this way, the "frames" of sequentially acquired data become "stacked" upon each other in chronological order. The lower half of Figure 5.1 also demonstrates that the resulting rows of data can be aligned vertically along a common fiducial point. In the example shown in Figure 5.1, the fiducial point used for the alignment is the peak of the QRS complex.

Several advantages of the SFD are immediately apparent. First, an entire analog display (e.g., an ECG complex) of any amplitude is now represented on a screen or a printout by a thin single line that is placed immediately below or above the previously acquired data. This permits one to display and review in a given space on a screen or printout much more information than would have been possible using the original analog representation of the data. Second, the color, grayscale, or pixel intensity coding of the information retains the amplitude and duration information that was present in the original analog display. Third, as Figure 5.2 demonstrates, the compactness and arrangement of the display of data not only increase the speed with which the data can be reviewed, but also permit easier identification of important patterns in the data that otherwise might not have been apparent. Figure 5.2 shows analog displays of sonar signals that were being used to detect a moving undersea object. Panels 1 and 2 show the traditional appearance of these signals as they sweep from the left to the right side of the screen and then disappear to accommodate the next series of sequentially recorded data. The transient nature of such displays of data that go by on a screen make it difficult to detect meaningful patterns in the signals. Also, the screen's "sweep speed" strongly affects both the accuracy and the time needed for the interpretation. A rapid sweep speed may cause the data to pass by before the observer can appropriately recognize patterns.

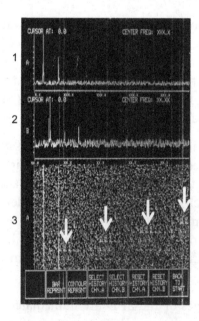

Fig. 5.2. Using the SFD to detect patterns in the data.

On the other hand, a slow sweep increases the time required to review all the data.

In contrast to Panels 1 and 2, Panel 3 of Figure 5.2 represents a SFD encoded by pixel brightness of a series of screens of data from Panel 1. In this case, the earliest recorded signals are at the bottom and the most recently recorded signals are at the top of Panel 3. Throughout most of the display on Panel 3, the accumulated recorded signals appear random. However, the four vertical arrows show distinct horizontal lines that represent reflected signals of a consistent type from an underwater object that is moving from left to right. In contrast to the traditional analog displays of data in Panels 1 and 2, the SFD makes it possible to identify the presence, direction, and (because of the known rate of acquisition of the data) the speed of the underwater object. It also allows the reviewer to see a large amount of data on a single screen.

An additional feature of an SFD displayed on a screen allows the user to click with a mouse on any part of the display, and it shows the more familiar traditional form of the analog signal represented by that part of the SFD. This capability further increases the ease with which SFD displays can be interpreted. In addition, each click of the computer's mouse on a portion of the SFD would show the date and time at which those data were recorded. This feature permits one to measure precisely the times at which any event of interest began and ended. Besides being presented on the screens of electronic monitors, one can choose to print or make screen shots of any portion of the display. This enables one to analyze data that had previously filled multiple screens, examine the data in sites remote from the electronic monitors and compile permanent records of the data that have been acquired.

Some features of the SFD resemble those of the color-coded Z score display that was discussed in Chapter 2. These similarities include the compression of analog data to the width of a single line and the use of color-coding to indicate the directions and magnitudes of changes in the recorded values of data. However, in contrast to the Z score display, the SFD has the following characteristics:

1. The SFD displays the measured values of the raw data rather than expressing each data point as the distance from the mean of a

comparison population of data in terms of the numbers of standard deviations of that population.

2. The color-coding in the SFD has nothing to do with the statistical significance of the displayed data.
3. Different parameters shown on the SFD are not all displayed on the same scale.
4. The SFD reveals changes in parameters throughout the entire range of their likely values, even if those changes are very small.
5. By showing this entire range of possible values, the SFD provides complete and accurate information about the amplitude and duration of each component of the analog waveform.

The ability of the SFD to reveal even small changes in analog displays of data, rather than only those that reach statistical significance, is very important and helps make the SFD useful for a number of possible applications. This is because many events of interest have expected ranges of duration and characteristic patterns of onset and offset. For example, in the monitoring of patients with known or suspected heart disease, one typically looks for displacement of the ST segments of the ECG complex as a diagnostic criterion for episodes of angina and myocardial infarction (MI). Compared to the maximum amplitude of the rest of the analog ECG signal, the magnitudes of diagnostically important ST segment displacement are usually very small. However, the temporal pattern they exhibit is diagnostically very important. The ST segment displacement associated with serious heart disease characteristically begins, gradually worsens, persists for at least several minutes, and then gradually resolves. The ability of the SFD to detect even very small magnitudes of ST segment change makes it possible to detect such a pattern of change. Even though the amount of displacement of the ST segments may never reach statistical significance, the observation of this temporal pattern in the appropriate clinical setting is of great diagnostic importance.

TESTING THE USEFULNESS OF THE SFD

The accuracy and efficiency of the SFD was tested by using it for the display and analysis of continuously recorded 24-h ambulatory ECG data. The test involved comparing the SFD's performance to that of the traditional method of reviewing such data. The subjects used in the study were 21 randomly selected patients consisting of 11 males and 10 females, ages 18–87 years (mean = 56) who had been cared for at an academic medical center in North Carolina. To evaluate the possible presence of arrhythmias and/or ischemic heart disease, each patient had undergone ambulatory two-channel ECG monitoring for 24 h. The data from each 24-h recording were then transferred to a computerized medical monitoring system that generated the SFD.

The traditional method of reviewing and interpreting the data consisted of the following: a cardiology technician examined the standard-ECG waveforms on the screen of an electronic ECG monitoring review station. The technicians' reviews of the data were augmented by sophisticated commercial diagnostic computer algorithms. The output of these diagnostic algorithms consisted of written descriptions of the algorithms' findings and graphs of any temporal changes in both heart rate and ST segment displacement. Each abnormality identified by the technician and/or the diagnostic algorithm during the 24-h recording was then presented for additional review by one of several cardiologists. For each of the patients, the reviewing cardiologist completed a diagnostic report based on the above information.

I tested the SFD method of reviewing and interpreting the data was as follows: after each patient's 24-h ECG data had been converted to the SFD format, I reviewed them on an electronic monitor. For these reviews of each patient's data, I was blinded to the standard ECG waveform, to the verbal and graphical output of the computer's diagnostic algorithm, and to the cardiologists' diagnostic reports. During these review of the data in the SFD format, I recorded both my diagnostic findings and the amount of time required to review each patient's entire 24-h record using the SFD. Finally, I compared the findings obtained by reviewing only the SFD to those recorded in the cardiologists' official diagnostic report. To determine whether I had correctly identified an abnormality using the SFD, I then examined the traditional analog ECG complex that corresponded to each pattern of interest revealed by the SFD.

Comparing the SFD to the original diagnostic reports showed that the SFD missed no abnormalities except for several clinically insignificant sinus pauses up to 2.8 s long in one patient. Conversely, the SFD detected a total of 9 episodes of consecutive ventricular beats (from 3 to 7 beats in duration) and a total of 10 episodes of sustained ST segment depression (from 1.5 min to 25 min in duration). All these episodes of sustained ventricular beats and ST segment depression were clinically significant, but the patients' official diagnostic reports did not mention any of them. Also, the SFD correctly revealed the artifactual nature of what the official reports had incorrectly identified as a total of four episodes of consecutive ventricular beats (reportedly from three to six beats in duration). The approximate typical time for the initial scanning of the standard ECG waveforms by the technician, plus their subsequent review by the cardiologist was 90 min. In contrast, the mean time required by me to review each 24-h ambulatory record using the SFD and to record my findings was 12 min, 32 s (range = 5 min, 13 s to 25 min, 30 s).

This study showed that the SFD is more accurate than the traditional method of analyzing 24-h ambulatory ECG data for identifying consecutive ventricular beats, ST segment displacement, and artifact. In addition, the mean time required to achieve this superior performance using the SFD is only about 14% of that typically required to analyze the same ECG data using the traditional method of analysis. The better performance of the SFD occurred despite the fact that the original, traditional analysis of the data had been assisted by the use of commercial diagnostic algorithms that had been written for the purpose of interpreting ambulatory ECG data.

The simultaneous improvement in diagnostic accuracy and efficiency is consistent with the features of the SFD. The traditional way of reviewing large numbers of serially acquired ECG complexes, i.e., observing the complexes as they scroll across a screen, is very laborious and often fails to reveal important patterns, as illustrated by Figure 5.2. An additional weakness of the traditional method of reviewing large amounts of continuous ECG data is the fact that these data are first screened by technicians before selected portions of the records are shown to the cardiologists who responsible for the final interpretations. Obviously, no matter how skilled the physicians are at interpreting ECG signals, they are able to see only those data that less highly trained technicians have chosen to show them. The technician's ability to appropriately select portions of the records for the cardiologists' review is impeded not only by their relative lack of expertise in electrocardiography, but also because of the monotony involved in reviewing a very large number of ECG complexes. This is further exacerbated by the fact that many of the important abnormalities (e.g., transient ST segment displacements of one or 2 mm) are so subtle that they can be hard to notice. For these reasons, even very experienced technicians are likely to miss some clinically significant events. In contrast, the ability of the SFD display to compress a large amount of data into a small space enables one to review effectively 24 or more hours of recorded ECG data much more rapidly than was previously possible. Importantly, this review of the data using the SFD does not require any prior screening by a technician. Therefore, the SFD provides full disclosure of the ECG data directly to the physician who must generate the diagnostic report. This full disclosure may well have contributed to the improved diagnostic accuracy for both arrhythmias and ischemia that the SFD exhibits.

Another factor that increases the accuracy of the SFD is the ability to use the computer's mouse to toggle between any portion of the SFD and the corresponding traditional ECG waveform as illustrated in Figure 5.3, where the familiar ECG waveform is located near the bottom of the screen. This toggling feature allows the users of the SFD to elucidate any changes in the pattern of a patient's SFD by instantly examining the more familiar analog ECG complex. It also quickly teaches the users what features of the standard ECG waveform the various types of patterns revealed by the SFD display represent. Such immediate instructional feedback is likely to increase the user's skill and efficiency as they accumulate experience with the SFD method.

Figure 5.3 illustrates a screen of some of the SFD data that were used in this study. There are four columns of sequentially acquired data that are aligned vertically, using the peak of the ECG R wave as a common fiducial point. Each separate column is located between a pair of thick black lines. The temporal sequence of the recordings is from top to bottom of the first column, then from top to bottom of the second column, and so on. In Figure 5.3, the white arrow on the SFD and the small rectangle on the traditional analog display at the bottom of the figure show the onset of an abrupt change in the appearance of the SFD. The SFD suggests that the ECG complexes that compose this small region have comparatively broad P waves, longer QT segments and intervals,

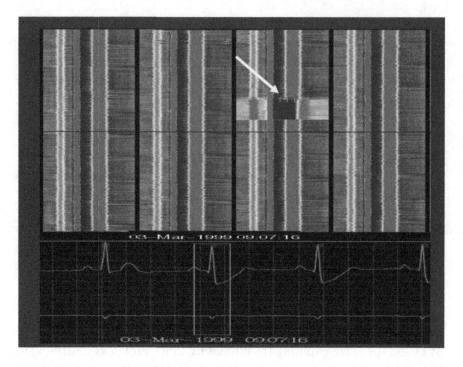

Fig. 5.3. SFD showing a sudden change in ECG morphology.

and lower T waves. The lower rectangle shows the traditional analog tracing at the point of transition to the above small region and confirms the morphological changes that the SFD suggest. The duration of the above episode lasted 15 s.

Figures 5.2 and 5.3 demonstrate that the ability of the SFD to compress a large number of sequentially acquired ECG data in a small space permits the reviewer to observe patterns that may not have been apparent from watching series of individual ECG complexes scroll across a screen. Furthermore, these patterns yield important quantitative information. The number of similar occurrences on one or more screens gives the frequency of an event during the period of recording. The duration of each episode of an event is proportional to the amount of vertical space that it occupies in a column. The magnitude of the change in amplitude of a portion of the ECG complex is proportional to the intensity of the change in color (or in the brightness of the pixels) that is associated with it. Finally, the rapidity with which any changes take place show whether they are gradual or instantaneous. The ability to identify such patterns can have considerable diagnostic importance. For example, ST segment displacement that begins, gradually worsens, and then gradually resolves over a period over a period of a few minutes is physiologically consistent with the known duration of myocardial ischemia. Therefore, such a pattern revealed by SFD would strongly suggest that the patient had had an episode of ischemia, whether symptomatic or "silent." Conversely, ST displacement that occurred and ended abruptly or persisted for a very brief period would not be consistent with the diagnosis of ischemia. Figure 5.3 illustrates an episode associated with marked ST depression. However, since this episode lasted only a few seconds and had a sudden onset and termination, it is extremely unlikely that ischemia was the cause of the observed change in this patient's ST segments. Figure 5.3 shows how easily the SFD simultaneously demonstrates the frequency, abruptness, direction, severity, and duration of an episode of ST displacement in a patient.

The facility with which the SFD can display such temporal information and also indicate specific patterns of the onset and offset of possible events of interest is very important. Such parameters can constitute the "fingerprints" of phenomena and events that we wish to detect. From previous observations, we often know that the entities that we wish to detect have a certain range of durations, specific directional characteristics (i.e., their values tend to be either higher or lower than the baseline condition), abrupt or gradual onsets and/or offsets, and expected ranges of severity. Its ability to provide information about such parameters reliably, even during the review of very large amounts of analog data, makes the SFD a powerful tool for analyzing computerized information.

In addition, after one identifies patterns of interest using the SFD, one can then quantify the relevant features of the ECG with great accuracy. This is because the system's computer has stored the digital data needed to generate the SFD and can therefore retrieve the precise computerized measurements of the analog signals associated with the identified patterns.

Besides using the SFD to detect and analyze ECG abnormalities in the initial evaluation of a patient, one can also use it to assess the safety and efficacy of therapeutic interventions in the daily management of patients and in the performance of clinical trials. Other investigators have used the traditional ambulatory ECG to evaluate the treatment of arrhythmias and ischemia. The full disclosure and ease of review of accumulated ECG data that the SFD provides makes it ideal for analyzing the large numbers of ambulatory ECGs that those clinical trials can generate.

The superiority of the SFD method for reviewing ECG data compared to the more traditional method that used sophisticated commercial diagnostic ECG algorithms again emphasizes an important point. This is the observation that the human eye and brain are extremely adept at quickly and accurately recognizing both simple and complex patterns. As the figures in this chapter have demonstrated, the SFD is a way of displaying even very large amounts of data in an intuitive and efficient way that easily reveals such patterns.

Although the present study specifically demonstrates the use of the SFD in ambulatory monitoring, it can be used with equal effectiveness for the monitoring of hospitalized patients, e.g., in coronary or intensive care units. In these settings, nurses or monitor technicians often try to detect clinically important changes in the tracings of multiple patients who are being monitored simultaneously. If a given ECG complex remains on the monitor screen for only a few seconds, it is very possible that some episodes of arrhythmia or ischemia will be missed. Even if all the patients' traditional ECG waveforms that had been obtained during a prolonged period were recorded, the task of subsequently reviewing them would be laborious and could diminish the ability of the professional staff to perform their other duties.

Using the SFD in conjunction with the real-time displays of monitored patients can facilitate the detection of clinically important abnormalities to help ensure that timely and effective therapeutic interventions are provided to the patients. Even if an important change in one or more clinical parameters in patients is not noted in real time, the SFD easily permits frequent retrospective reviews of the monitored data that had been recorded. Frequent reviews would minimize the amount of time between the actual occurrence of a clinical event and any intervention that would be appropriate for that event. Furthermore, the demonstrated ability of the SFD to show important details about the changes in the monitored parameters would have additional diagnostic value.

Another application of the SFD is the "sleep study," i.e., polysomnography. Sleep studies are performed to investigate the presence, severity, and nature of the abnormalities associated with obstructive or central sleep apnea. During these studies, a variety of clinical parameters are continuously recorded, usually for a period of several hours. These parameters consist of some combination of the following: the ECG signal, oxygen saturation, carbon dioxide levels, respiratory rate, chest movements, activity of leg muscles, body temperature, and jaw muscle tone. The SFD would be an ideal method for displaying and analyzing the effects of sleep on each of them.

Regardless of its specific application, a particularly important feature of the SFD is that it permits very efficient comprehensive review of the data. This comprehensiveness helps ensure that caregivers didn't miss anything concerning the clinical parameters that were being monitored. The comprehensiveness of data review provided by the SFD also permits the caregivers to assess accurately whether any possible therapeutic interventions were effective. Did the administration of an antianginal drug reduce the number and severity of episodes of ischemia? Did intensified treatment of heart failure decrease the frequency and severity of reductions in oxygen saturation? In addition to its benefits for patients' daily care, such comprehensiveness would be a valuable feature when conducting clinical research. Such research could be in the context of either academic work or by pharmaceutical companies in the course of the development of new drugs.

USING THE SFD ON THE PERSONAL COMPUTER

Whereas companies that manufacture devices that store and display computerized data can incorporate the SFD in commercial devices, individual users can also generate many of the same features of the SFD using their personal computers. The following is an example of the creation of a SFD using the spreadsheet program Microsoft Excel.

In this example, digital ECG data were downloaded from a commercial ECG machine. The downloaded data used in this example were from each of 1079 patients whose diagnoses had been established by cardiac catheterization. Of the 1079 patients, 474 were normal, 341 had inferior MI, and 274 had anterior MI. Inferior MI and anterior MI are each common types of heart attacks. The data recorded from each patient consisted of the cardiac voltages in microvolts that had been recorded in ECG standard Lead aVF during the ECG QRS complex. The QRS complex is that part of the ECG signal that shows the heart's electrical activity during activation (depolarization) of the ventricles. These voltages had been sequentially recorded at 4-ms intervals during the QRS. Relevant to this example of the SFD, a common ECG feature of inferior MI is that the QRS complex in lead aVF often begins with a prolonged downward deflection, i.e., a wide Q wave is present. Such prominently downward initial QRS displacement in lead aVF is not a typical feature in either normal patients or patients with anterior MI [7,8].

The downloaded QRS voltages were copied to Excel and arranged in the spreadsheet, as illustrated by Table 5.1.

In Table 5.1, the first row of numbers designates the labels of the columns under which the 4-ms samples of ECG data are listed. For example, under "4" in the first row are listed the voltages recorded at 4 ms after the onset of the QRS complex. Each row of data in this matrix contains the data for each of the 1079 patients. These patients are grouped together for each of the three diagnostic categories in the study – normal, inferior MI, and anterior MI.

The data in the matrix could be color-coded by coloring red all the cells that contain positive numbers and by coloring blue all the cells that contain negative numbers. Therefore, on a color screen or printout, the red cells would represent upward deflections of the corresponding part of the analog QRS complex, and the blue cells would represent downward deflections of the corresponding part of the QRS. The heights of all the spreadsheet's data-containing rows were then compressed from their default value of 12.75 units to a new value of 1.0. Color-coding can be done by using the Conditional Formatting option of Excel as described in Chapter 2 on Z scores.

Table 5.1 Illustration of ECG QRS Voltage Matrix in Lead aVF												
Patient No.	4	8	12	16	20	24	28	32	36	40	44	48	52
1	−4	9	58	87	200	288	371	483	483	268	87	−73	−190
2	48	107	151	122	34	−29	−92	−117	−112	−151	−302	−454	−458
3	0	4	−4	−29	−83	−136	−151	−180	−166	−166	−195	48	107
4	−4	−43	−83	−73	−4	73	244	415	454	380	375	493	546
5	−14	14	29	34	19	39	73	141	185	332	380	278	195

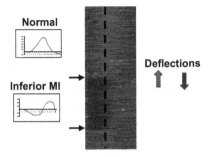

Fig. 5.4. SFD used for ECG diagnosis.

Figure 5.4 shows the SFD of this set of ECG that was generated using the spreadsheet software. In Figure 5.4, the vertical dashed black line indicates the demarcation between the 40 ms and the 44 ms sampling interval. The upper horizontal black arrow shows the point of demarcation between the normal group and the inferior MI group of patients. The lower horizontal black arrow shows the point of demarcation between the inferior MI group and the anterior MI group of patients. To the left of the colored SFD in Figure 5.4 are boxes that show two ECG waveforms. The upper waveform shows the QRS complex of one of the patients in the normal group and was created by choosing one of the rows of data in the normal group and then using the graphing function of the spreadsheet program to produce a line graph of the data points in that row. The lower ECG waveform was produced in a similar way, using a row of data points in one the patients in the inferior MI group. The correspondence between these sample ECG waveforms and the SFD is important. The shortness of the initial blue segments that would be observed in a color display of the SFD of the normal patients corresponds to the very minor downward deflection in the upper line graph. However, the much longer initial blue segments in a color display of the inferior MI subgroup corresponds to the much more prominent initial downward deflection in the lower line graph. Once again, examination of the SFD permits one to accurately infer the details of the traditional analog representation the data. Figure 5.4 also demonstrates how the SFD improves the efficiency of the interpretation of analog data. This is because the entire column of data shown in Figure 5.4 is a meaningful representation of the ECG QRS waveforms of the entire group of 1079 patients.

Of course, in the SFD shown in Figure 5.4, the patients had already been aggregated in the three diagnostic groups – normal, inferior MI, and anterior MI. This aggregation among the three diagnostic groups had been done deliberately for the purposes demonstrating the SFD's ability to discriminate among diagnostic categories. A more realistic diagnostic situation would exist if the patients had not been aggregated in this way, but instead had been arranged randomly with respect to their diagnoses. In the latter case, one could have identified each of the patients with inferior MI by scrolling down the SFD and selecting each row that began with a prolonged blue segment.

On the other hand, deliberately aggregating the patients before examining the SFD could have served another important purpose. Continuing with the present diagnostic example, let us imagine that the ECG manifestations of inferior MI were not yet known. We could have produced an SFD of the patients aggregated by diagnoses that were determined by tests independent of the ECG, just as is shown in Figure 5.4. The SFD would have shown us very quickly that prolonged initial blue segments characterize most of the rows that represent the inferior MI patients. Knowing how this particular SFD was generated, we would therefore have learned that the presence of prolonged downward deflection of the initial part of the QRS complex in lead aVF is a characteristic ECG feature exhibited by patients with inferior MI.

The features of the SFD illustrated in Figure 5.4 have an additional important application. Figure 5.4 shows aggregations of data that are grouped by diagnostic classifications. With equal ease, the SFD can identify changes in data that are grouped with respect to the times at which they occur. Time series are the measured values of data points that have been made sequentially during a particular period. Temporal changes in parameters that are being measured would be revealed in a manner similar to that shown in Figure 5.4. As emphasized in Chapter 3, analyses of time series of data are very important in many fields and constitute ideal applications of the SFD.

REFERENCES

[1] Corder MP, Monaco JL, Kraf T, Levin RI. The introduction of ambulatory electrocardiographic monitoring for the diagnosis and management of myocardial ischemia. Am J Med Qual 1997;12(3):169–74.

[2] Benhorin J, Pinsker G, Moriel M, Gavish A, Tzivoni D, Stern S. Ischemic threshold during two exercise testing protocols and during ambulatory electrocardiographic monitoring. J Am Coll Cardiol 1993;22(3):671–7.

[3] Tomita F. Characteristics and clinical significance of silent myocardial ischemia during ambulatory electrocardiographic monitoring in patients with ischemic heart disease. Hokkaido Igaku Zasshi 1990;65(6):583–94.

[4] Di Marco JP, Philbrick JT. Use of ambulatory electrocardiographic (Holter) monitoring. Ann Intern Med 1990;113(1):53–68.

[5] Deedwania PC, Carbajal EV. Exercise test predictors of ambulatory silent ischemia during daily life in stable angina pectoris. Am J Cardiol 1990;66(17):1151–6.

[6] Grauer K, Leytem B. A systematic approach to Holter monitor interpretation. Am Fam Physician 1992;45(4):1641–8.

[7] Warner RA, Hill N, Sheehe P, Mookherjee S, Fruehan CT, Smulyan H. Improved electrocardiographic criteria for the diagnosis of inferior myocardial infarction. Circulation 1982;66:422–8.

[8] Warner RA, Hill NE. Optimized electrocardiographic criteria for prior inferior and an anterior myocardial infarction. J Electrocardiol 2012;45:209–13.

CHAPTER 6

Effective Methods for Analyzing Digital Data

Much of this book has addressed the importance of displaying analog information in ways that are both accurate and intuitive. Such displays permit one to see meaningful patterns in the information, even when performing comprehensive reviews of large sets of data. When such patterns suggest the presence of a phenomenon of interest, it is often desirable to develop precise criteria for identifying it. For example, various analog displays of data described in this book have shown that groups of patients with the type of heart attack called prior inferior myocardial infarction (MI) exhibit a particular pattern. Compared to normal subjects, patients with inferior MI abnormality tend to have more negative deflections in the initial portions of their QRS complexes in standard ECG lead aVF. That is certainly an important observation. However, when we turn to the task of diagnosing a prior inferior MI in an individual patient, we need much more precise diagnostic criteria, i.e., specific rules for making the diagnosis. For example, based on the above general pattern shown by the analog displays, we might hypothesize that there is a quantitative relationship between voltage negativity early in the QRS complex of lead aVF and the likelihood that a given patient has a prior inferior MI. If this hypothesis is correct, then exactly what value of voltage negativity in this part of the ECG should we use to either make or exclude the diagnosis of prior inferior MI in a given patient? An accurate answer to this question would provide us with a precise quantitative diagnostic criterion for this important abnormality of the heart.

There are two different approaches to addressing such a quantitative question. In the first, we can treat Q wave duration in lead aVF as a continuous parameter. That means there is a relatively smooth range of values of early QRS voltages from strongly positive to strongly negative. Our task then would be to pick the exact point in this range of values that produces what we believe to be the best diagnostic performance for detecting prior inferior MI.

Alternatively, we could use early QRS voltage negativity in lead aVF as a dichotomous parameter. A dichotomous parameter provides a single yes or no answer to the question of whether or not a hypothesis is correct – in this case, whether a particular patient has a prior inferior MI. In this approach, we would choose a single threshold value of voltage negativity. Any ECG whose early QRS voltage in lead aVF that chosen threshold value of negativity would be said to be consistent with prior MI. Any ECG that did not reach that threshold value of negativity of the early QRS complex in lead aVF value would be said not to be consistent with prior inferior MI.

Whether we use diagnostic parameters as continuous or as dichotomous variables, we must decide what constitutes an optimal level of sensitivity or specificity. Such a choice is necessary because there is always an inverse relationship between the sensitivity and specificity of a test. In the present example, we have hypothesized that the more negative the early ECG QRS voltages are in lead aVF, the more likely it is that prior inferior MI is present. Therefore, if we choose a relatively less negative value of such voltages as our diagnostic threshold value, we will have chosen a diagnostic criterion with relatively high sensitivity and relatively low specificity. This is because a less negative threshold value would identify more ECGs as showing prior inferior MI than would a more stringent threshold value. Any ECG thus identified as positive for this diagnosis must be either a true positive (TP) or a false positive (FP). Detecting more TPs would increase the test's sensitivity, and simultaneously selecting additional ECGs that are FPs would decrease the test's specificity.

Conversely, choosing a more negative, and therefore more stringent, diagnostic threshold value would identify a higher proportion of ECGs as negative for prior MI. The correct identification of more actual noncases by this more stringent criterion would increase diagnostic specificity. However, the incorrect labeling of actual cases as noncases would decrease diagnostic sensitivity.

This book has shown various ways in which numerical data can be used to produce analog displays that show meaningful patterns in the data. We can also use the same digital data to maximize the precision and usefulness of the information that these patterns provide. For continuous parameters, an excellent method for developing precise quantitative criteria for identifying phenomena of interest is to construct receiver operating characteristic (ROC) curves. The ROC curve was developed during World War II to permit the British to better identify incoming German planes using radar. The British military had learned that their radar equipment was very good at detecting enemy airplanes. However, if the settings that the British were using made the radar too sensitive, the radar detected too many FPs because besides identifying actual airplanes, it also incorrectly identified flights of birds as airplanes. On the other hand, reducing the sensitivity of the radar settings too much would produce too many false negatives (FNs) because the equipment would miss signals that actually represented enemy aircraft. The method that was developed at this time to help choose the correct radar settings was the ROC curve.

Similarly, in detecting other phenomena of interest, e.g., the presence of a particular disease, it is often necessary to choose threshold values that produce the desired combination of sensitivity and specificity. Figure 6.1 shows an example of an ROC curve. The phenomenon to

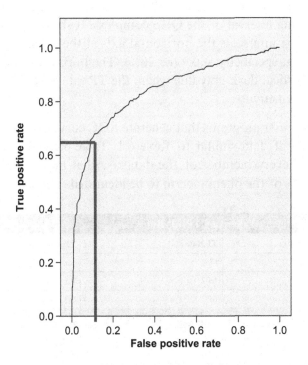

Fig. 6.1. ROC curve for prior inferior MI QRS voltage in ECG lead aVF at 32 ms.

be detected is prior inferior MI and the parameter used for its detection is the recorded voltage in microvolts recorded at the 32-ms sample after the onset of the QRS complex in lead aVF.

As Figure 6.1 shows, the Y-axis of the ROC curve shows the TP rate. This is the same as diagnostic sensitivity and indicates the proportion of the diagnoses of prior inferior MI made by this criterion that are correct. The X-axis of the ROC curve shows the FP rate, i.e., the proportion of all the noncases of prior inferior MI that this criterion incorrectly identified as being actual cases. The FP rate is the same as 1.0 minus the specificity. For example if the FP rate is 0.3, it means that the specificity = 1.0 − 0.3 = 0.7. The ROC curve itself is the curved line that is convex to the left and upward. The ROC curve is an XY plot of the TP and FP rates associated with the value of each data point that is in either the normal group or in the prior inferior MI group.

The vertical and horizontal dark gray lines superimposed on the graph illustrate how the ROC curve can reveal the diagnostic performance of a proposed criterion (in this case the recorded voltage at the 32nd sampling interval of the QRS complex). It shows that the vertical dark gray line intersects the horizontal axis at the point where FP rate is 0.10, i.e., at specificity = 0.9 (or 90%). The horizontal dark gray line abuts the vertical dark gray line where the TP rate is about 0.67, i.e., at about 67% sensitivity.

The computer programs that generate ROC curves also typically produce a table of data similar to Table 6.1. Table 6.1 shows the TP and FP rates of every member of the database that includes all the cases and noncases of the phenomenon to be identified. These accompanying

Table 6.1 Parameter Values and TP/FP Rates		
Parameter Values	TP Rate (%)	FP Rate (%)
−16.5	63.6	9.1
−11.5	64.8	9.1
−6.5	65.7	9.3
−2.0	66.6	10.3
2.0	68.0	11.2
6.5	68.0	11.9
11.5	68.3	12.7

tables therefore obviate the need to merely estimate diagnostic sensitivities and specificities as shown by the dark gray lines in Figure 6.1. Instead, these tables provide the precise values of sensitivity and specificity. Furthermore, each row of the table includes the value that is associated with each listed sensitivity and specificity. As is illustrated in Table 6.1, the row that is highlighted in dark gray shows that at the 32nd sampling interval of the ECG QRS complex of lead aVF, a threshold value of −2.0 mV is associated is with 66.6% sensitivity, and $100 - 10.3 = 89.7\%$ specificity for prior inferior MI.

There are many available computer programs that produce ROC curves, and each program is accompanied by instructions for using it. Some of these programs can be downloaded at no cost from the Internet. To use these programs, one only needs a set of data that contains the measurements of a parameter that is relevant to identifying the phenomenon for which one wants to develop an identifying criterion. This set of data must designate which of the data points are associated with cases and which are the ones associated with noncases of the phenomenon of interest. A very useful feature of good programs that generate ROC curves is that they permit digital data from many different sources (including spreadsheet programs) to be downloaded to them.

A parameter that is often used in the analysis of ROC curves is the "area under the curve," often abbreviated as "AUC." The greater the area under an ROC curve, the greater is the ability of the parameter represented by that curve to discriminate in a general way between the cases and the noncases of the phenomenon that one is trying to detect. However, people who analyze data are often interested in discriminating between the cases and noncases of a phenomenon in much more than only a general way. For example, those who develop criteria that are intended to identify specific phenomena often have in mind what they consider to be an "acceptable" FP rate. This is to prevent the criteria from producing what the users of the data consider to be a desired maximum proportion of incorrect identifications of the phenomenon. At the same time, a feature of a good criterion for identifying a phenomenon is that while minimizing the rate of FPs that it produces, it still maintains a relatively high TP rate. After all, the underlying purpose of trying to develop the criterion is to permit as many accurate detections of the phenomenon as possible.

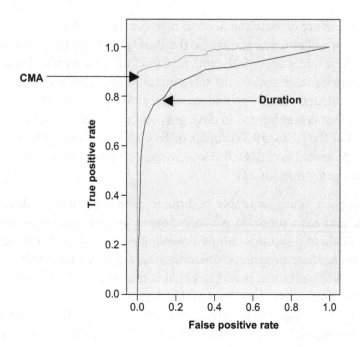

Fig. 6.2. ROC curves for prior inferior MI lead aVF Q-wave duration versus 10-s CMA of Q-wave duration.

For these reasons, the author believes that there are more important features of an ROC curve than its AUC. These features include the rapidity with which the initial portion of the curve rises and for how long that rapid rise is maintained. Figure 6.2 demonstrates this by comparing two separate ROC curves. Each of the ROC curves in Figure 6.2 portrays the diagnostic performances of two different parameters for diagnosing prior inferior MI. As Figure 6.2 shows, one of the diagnostic parameters is the duration of ECG Q waves in standard lead aVF. The other curve in Figure 6.2 is the parameter 10-s central moving average (CMA) that was described in detail in Chapter 3. First, the ability to superimpose two or more ROC curves on the same graph is a powerful feature for making direct visual comparisons of the diagnostic abilities of different diagnostic parameters. Second, comparing the two curves shows the importance of both the abruptness with which the initial part of an ROC curve rises and for how long this rapid rise is sustained.

Figure 6.2 shows that the ROC curve of the Q wave duration data in lead aVF rises straight up for a brief period and then continues to rise less and less rapidly throughout the remainder of the display. This pattern means that as the Q-wave duration parameter identifies more and more TPs, it does so at the cost of also acquiring more FPs. In contrast, the ROC curve of the 10-s CMA data rises vertically for a much longer period before it starts to slope toward the right. This means that in comparison to the Q-wave duration parameter, the 10-s CMA parameter identifies many more TPs before it starts to also identify any FPs. To quantify this comparison of the two parameters, the sensitivity of Q-wave duration for prior inferior MI at 100% diagnostic specificity is only 11% and this was attained at a threshold value of 73 ms. However, the sensitivity of the 10-s CMA for prior inferior MI at 100% diagnostic specificity is much higher at 90%, and this was attained at a lower threshold value of only 28 ms.

Just as ROC curves represent an excellent method for developing and evaluating continuous parameters for the testing of hypotheses, the use of the chi square test is appropriate for hypotheses that involve dichotomous data. The chi square test is a technique for comparing different proportionalities. For example, one might hypothesize that Observation A is present in a higher proportion of the instances when Phenomenon X is present than it is when Phenomenon X is absent. If the available data confirm this hypothesis, then one would be justified in considering the presence of Observation A as a useful criterion for identifying the presence Phenomenon X. In this example, Observation A is either present or not present. Therefore, Observation A is a dichotomous criterion for deciding in a given set of circumstances whether or not Phenomenon X is present.

Table 6.2 illustrates the use of the chi square analysis to determine the statistical significance of differences in proportionality when evaluating dichotomous parameters. As was the case in the previously described

Table 6.2 Dichotomous Criterion for Prior Inferior MI			
Lead aVF Q-Wave ≥30 ms	Inferior MI Absent	Inferior MI Present	Total
No	467 (94.0%)	101 (27.6%)	568 (65.8%)
Yes	30 (6.0%)	265 (72.4%)	295 (34.2%)
Total	497 (100%)	366 (100%)	863 (100%)

use of ROC curves, we are evaluating the use of an ECG criterion to determine the presence of prior inferior MI in patients. The dichotomous criterion that we are evaluating at this point is the observed presence of a Q wave $\geq$30 ms in duration in standard ECG lead aVF. Table 6.2 shows the distributions of this ECG finding in the normal patients and in the patients with independent evidence of prior MI.

As shown in Table 6.2, a total of 863 patients are included in the study. Of these, 497 are normal (designated in Table 6.2 as "Inferior MI Absent"), and 366 have prior inferior MI. Among the 497 normal patients, only 6.0% meet the criterion of having a Q-wave duration in lead aVF $\geq$30 ms. In contrast, 72.4% of the patients with prior inferior MI meet this criterion. Therefore, the proportion of patients with Q waves in lead aVF $\geq$30 ms is 12 times greater in patients with prior inferior MI than it is in patients without prior inferior MI. This difference in proportions revealed by the data in Table 6.2 suggests that the presence of Q waves $\geq$30 ms duration in lead aVF is a very good criterion for testing the hypothesis that a patient has inferior MI.

To formally test the hypothesis that the observed difference in proportions shown in Table 6.2 is statistically significant, one can use chi-square analysis. There are many computer programs, including free ones that can be downloaded from the Internet, that calculate chi square values and the P values associated with them. In the present example, one simply enters the appropriate raw numerical data from Table 6.2 into a 2 × 2 matrix and instructs the program to provide the result of the calculation:

$$467 \quad 101$$
$$30 \quad 265$$

In this case, the result of the calculation is: Chi square = 413, $P < 8.14 \times 10^{-92}$.

This calculated result confirms that a Q wave in ECG lead aVF whose duration $\geq$ 30 ms is an excellent diagnostic criterion for discriminating between people with versus those prior inferior MI.

One must often choose among different possible ways of testing hypotheses, e.g., whether a particular phenomenon of interest is present. The question then becomes, which is the diagnostic criterion that works the best? Figure 6.2 shows that for continuous parameters, one may superimpose and visually compare ROC curves. One may also compare tests by comparing their sensitivities and specificities, but since these measurements vary inversely, the choice of whether to emphasize sensitivity or specificity is frequently arbitrary. A commonly used way of evaluating tests for various phenomena is to calculate their positive and negative predictive values given these formulae:

$$\text{Positive predictive value} = \frac{TP}{TP+FP}$$

$$\text{Negative predictive value} = \frac{TN}{TN+FN}$$

However, as will be discussed in the next chapter on conditional probability, the proportions of TPs versus FPs and of TNs versus FNs depend heavily on the prevalence in the population of the phenomenon that one is trying to identify. Therefore, since one frequently uses tests in populations in which the respective prevalences are both variable and uncertain, the usefulness of using the calculated positive and negative predictive values to compare tests is limited.

Much better parameters for directly comparing tests that might be used to identify phenomena are the positive and the negative likelihood ratios:

$$\text{Positive likelihood ratio} = \frac{\% \, \text{Sensitivity}}{100 - \% \, \text{Specificity}}$$

Although opinions vary concerning the correct formula for the negative likelihood ratio, the one that the author has found most useful is:

$$\text{Negative likelihood ratio} = \frac{\% \, \text{Specificity}}{100 - \% \, \text{Sensitivity}}$$

The positive likelihood ratio expresses the ability of a test to rule in the presence of a phenomenon of interest, regardless of the prevalence of that phenomenon in the population being tested. The negative likelihood ratio expresses the ability of a test to rule out the presence of a phenomenon of interest and is also independent of the prevalence of that phenomenon in the population being tested.

Related to the above, there is a less widely used parameter that is also independent of prevalence, and that is intended to express a test's overall (both rule in and rule out) ability to correctly identify a phenomenon of interest. These are the relative odds:

$$\text{Relative odds} = \frac{\%\text{Sensitivity} \times \%\text{Specificity}}{(100 - \%\text{Sensitivity}) \times (100 - \%\text{Specificity})}$$

Positive likelihood ratio × Negative likelihood ratio

For example, if a test for the presence of a phenomenon of interest has a sensitivity of 60% and a specificity of 90%:

$$\text{Positive likelihood ratio} = \frac{60}{100 - 90} = \frac{60}{10} = 6.0$$

$$\text{Negative likelihood ratio} = \frac{90}{100 - 60} = \frac{90}{40} = 2.25$$

$$\text{Relative Odds} = \frac{60 \times 90}{(100 - 60)(100 - 90)} = \frac{5400}{40 \times 10} = \frac{5400}{400}$$

$$= 13.5 \text{ or, alternatively}, 6.0 \times 2.25 = 13.5$$

This chapter and the ones that preceded it demonstrate an important aspect of the power and usefulness of computerized data. The digital information acquired by a wide variety of devices and then stored in the electronic memories of computers can be used to generate meaningful visual patterns. This process takes advantage of the great ability of humans to recognize such patterns, even when the patterns exist in the midst of the "noise" associated with very large quantities of other data. The recognition of these patterns can take place regardless of the method that was used to produce them, e.g., the previously discussed color-coded Z scores, moving averages, composite analog displays, or stacked frame displays.

Then, once the meaningful patterns have been recognized, the same digital data that had been used to create the displays can be analyzed in great detail. This entire process permits us to learn as much as possible from the information that has been made available to us and to increase the depth and breadth of our understanding of the world around us.

CHAPTER 7

The Importance of Conditional Probability

PROBABILITY AND CONDITIONAL PROBABILITY

Probability in general expresses the likelihood that some particular thing is true, e.g., that a patient has a particular disease or that an economic recession will occur within the next 12 months. In conditional probability, literally another relevant "condition" is specified, and this added condition changes one's belief about the overall assessment of the final probability. For instance, let's say we are trying to decide whether statement or belief A is true, and in addition to A, there is also a set of circumstances B. A question that we might ask is, "What is the likelihood that A is true given the condition that B is also true?" An alternative form of the same question is, "What is the probability of A *conditional* upon the truth of B?"

In the above, B can be considered a background condition that provides the general context in which one evaluates the truth of a specific statement or belief. For example, let us say that a certain person makes a particular statement, and we are trying decide if that statement is true. We also learn that the person who made the statement in question has often been shown in the past to be deceitful. This history of deceitfulness by the person who had made the specific statement under consideration is now a background condition that we would probably use in deciding whether his current statement is true. More generally, and in the language of conditional probability, we would ask, "What is the likelihood that this person's current statement is true, conditional upon the previously observed deceitfulness of that person?"

It is enormously important to consider conditional probability when analyzing data. The following is a dramatic but realistic example of the importance of background conditions when evaluating evidence. Consider a blood test for prostate cancer that groups of respected researchers have declared is 75% specific for prostate cancer.

This means that for a patient who has a positive result on this test, one can reasonably conclude that there is a 75% chance prostate cancer is present and a 25% chance that the positive result is due to something other than prostate cancer. However, in a particular patient who had a positive result on this prostate cancer blood test, it is then revealed that the patient from whom this sample of blood was drawn is a woman. In this example, if one considered only the result of the blood test, one would believe that there was three chances out of four the patient had prostate cancer. However, by learning the background condition, i.e., that this patient is a female, the likelihood that prostate cancer is present dropped from 75% to 0%. No matter how accurate a test for a disease might otherwise be, a positive result on that test obviously cannot be a true positive (TP) if the patient does not possess the organ that is subject to that disease.

The principles of conditional probability can be used in many contexts and can be illustrated readily by considering their importance in questions concerning the general accuracy of medical diagnostic testing. To do this, we must first define several terms that are relevant to the testing of patients for any disease:

- True Positive (TP) – The test says that a patient has the disease, and the patient actually does have the disease, i.e., the test is correct.
- False Positive (FP) – The test says that a patient has the disease, but the patient does not actually have the disease, i.e., the test is incorrect.
- True Negative (TN) – The test says that a patient does not have the disease, and the patient actually does not have the disease, i.e., the test is correct.
- False Negative (FN) – The test says that a patient does not have the disease, but the patient does actually have the disease, i.e., the test is incorrect.
- Prevalence – This is the proportion (typically expressed as a percentage) of the population that has a particular disease. It is commonly confused with incidence, which is the rate at which the members of a population acquire a particular disease.
- Sensitivity (of a test) – The percentage of actual cases of a disease in a population that the test has identified as cases, i.e., the percentage

of all the positive results of a test that are TPs. It can be calculated using the formula:

$$\text{Sensitivity} = \frac{TP}{TP + FN}$$

- Specificity (of a test) – The percentage of actual noncases of a disease in a population that the test has identified as noncases, i.e., the percentage of all negative results of a test that are TNs. It can be expressed by the formula:

$$\text{Specificity} = \frac{TN}{TN + FP}$$

However, there is a crucial fact about diagnostic testing that unfortunately is frequently ignored:

The accuracy of any test for a disease is heavily influenced by the prevalence of that disease in the population being tested.

Specifically:

- The greater the prevalence of the disease in the population being tested, the more likely it is that a positive result given by the diagnostic test is a TP, rather than a FP.
- Conversely, the lower the prevalence of the disease in the population being tested, the more likely it is that a negative result given by the test is a TN, rather than a FN.

The following example demonstrates the importance of the prevalence of a disease on the results of testing for that disease:

A diagnostic test has 60% sensitivity and 90% specificity for disease X. This test is given to the members of each of two populations:

1. Population A consists of 1000 people in which the prevalence of disease X is 50%.

The 50% prevalence means that in population A, 500 people have disease X, and 500 do not.

Since the test for disease X has 60% sensitivity, it will correctly identify 500 × 0.6 = 300 of the people who have the disease, i.e.,

Table 7.1 Effects of Prevalence on the Accuracy of Tests							
Population	Total	TP	FP	TP/FP	TN	FN	TN/FN
A: prevalence = 50%	1000	300	50	6.00	450	200	2.25
B: prevalence = 10%	1000	60	90	0.67	810	200	4.05
Test with 60% sensitivity/90% specificity.							

produce <u>300</u> TPs. It will also incorrectly say that $500 \times 0.4 = 200$ do not have the disease, i.e., produce 200 FNs.

Also, since the test for disease X has 90% specificity, it will produce $500 \times 0.9 = 450$ TNs and $500 \times 0.1 = 50$ FPs.

2. Population B consists of 1000 people in which the prevalence of disease X is only 10%.

The 10% prevalence means that in population B, 100 people have disease X and 900 do not.

Since the test for disease X has 60% sensitivity, it will produce $100 \times 0.6 = 60$ TPs and $100 \times 0.4 = 40$ FNs.

Also, since the test for disease X has 90% specificity, it will produce $900 \times 0.9 = 810$ TNs and $900 \times 0.1 = 90$ FPs.

Table 7.1 summarizes these results.

Table 7.1 shows that in the group with the higher prevalence of the disease, a positive result on the test for the disease is much more likely to be a correct result than it is to be an incorrect result by a ratio of 6:1. Conversely, in the group with the lower prevalence of the disease, a positive result on the same test is less likely to be a correct result than it is to be an incorrect result, by a ratio of 2:3. The reverse of this phenomenon is true regarding identification of noncases of disease X. Table 7.1 shows that in population B with a lower prevalence of disease X, the same diagnostic test yields a higher ratio of correct to incorrect results it does in population A – 4.05:1 versus 2.25:1.

Although the principles of conditional probability can be used in many fields, medical diagnostic testing is an excellent paradigm for thinking about conditional probability. In the example of the positive test for prostate cancer as well as in the example of testing for disease X in two different populations, we see the importance of disease prevalence as a "background condition" for diagnosing a particular disease. A relevant background condition provides important context in which the results of diagnostic testing should be interpreted. In the example of the aforementioned test for prostate cancer, "male sex" is the background condition that makes any realistic interpretation of this particular cancer test possible. In the example of diagnosing disease X, the prevalence of disease in populations A versus B heavily determined the reliability of the same test for this disease.

In the field of conditional probability, the word "testing" most generally refers to the testing of hypotheses. In medicine, the hypothesis to be tested may be that a particular patient has a certain disease. In economics, the hypothesis may be that a major recession will soon occur. In marketing, the hypothesis may be that customers may find a particular set of a product's features especially attractive.

The notion of hypothesis testing is so prevalent in the field of conditional probability that one often encounters the terms "pre-test" and "post-test" probability. If a test is performed to evaluate the likelihood that a certain hypothesis is true, the result of that test is called the post-test or posterior probability. This is because the resultant probability was estimated after (post or posterior to) the performance of the test. However, the background conditions under which the test was performed existed before the test was conducted. Therefore, considering these background conditions can yield a pre-test or prior probability that the hypothesis is correct. In the case of the hypothetical test for prostate cancer, learning of the background condition that the patient is a female gave a pre-test probability of zero for the hypothesis that the patient has prostate cancer. The examples given show that relevant background conditions provide the context in which specific tests for a certain hypothesis are interpreted. It is therefore extremely important to remember that to best determine the truth or falsity of any hypothesis, one should consider both the relevant prior and posterior probabilities. One must evaluate not only the direct evidence that might support the hypothesis, but also the indirect background or contextual information that is available.

Certainly, the effect of considering pre-test conditions need not be as dramatic as the example of a woman with a positive test for prostate cancer. For example, the prevalence of many diseases varies with age. If one considers a disease whose prevalence increases with age, a positive diagnostic test for that disease is less likely to be a correct result in a young adult than it is in an elderly person. Also, various companies and healthcare institutions sometimes market "screening tests" that are intended to detect various diseases, hopefully in their early stages. These tests may consist of such things as blood tests, imaging studies, breathing tests, and ECGs. However, since they are screening tests, they are very often administered to people who have no clinical manifestations of the diseases that they are intended to detect. This is in contrast to diagnostic tests that have been ordered for patients who have signs and symptoms that suggest the presence of a specific disease. In other words, many screening tests are administered to people with a very low prevalence (i.e., prior probability) of disease in contrast to symptomatic patients who would have a much higher prevalence of the disease being tested for.

Considering the principles of conditional probability can have dramatic effects in many fields. For example, a team of geologists may notice that one of the seismographs in a location that they have been studying has shown a sudden increase in seismic activity in that region. Upon studying the seismographic records, the geologists initially conclude that this new pattern of recorded vibrations in the earth is probably the precursor to a major earthquake. However, the geologists then learn that because of road building activity near that same seismograph, construction workers have been using dynamite to clear a path for a new road. This newly acquired knowledge of the road building activity constitutes a background condition that would probably cause the geologists to reevaluate their original hypothesis that a major earthquake that region was likely to occur in the near future.

The effects of specifying additional conditions on the final probability of the truth of a given belief (e.g., that a patient has a certain disease or that an earthquake will occur soon) are not surprising. After all, specifying such conditions means that one is adding more information to help decide the truth or falsity of a belief or assertion. For example, in the case involving the blood test for prostate cancer described above, having the information that the test for cancer was positive led to one entirely reasonable interpretation of this test. However, providing the additional information about the sex of the patient led to a very different and much more accurate conclusion about the patient. As long as the added information is relevant, correct, and nonredundant, having more information rather than less makes it easier to reliably determine whether a belief about something is true or false.

Actually, all of us frequently use the basic ideas of conditional probability in an informal way. For example, we know that its unreasonable to expect that the statements made by people are always dispassionate. Our evaluation of the underlying circumstances may affect our assessment of the likely truth of what a given person says. Do we tend to accept uncritically a salesman's description of a product when we know that he is trying to sell that product to us? Do we sometimes question the promises that politicians make while they running for office? Knowing the accuracy of so many of the predictions of modern science, are we more predisposed to accept scientific rather than supernatural explanations of phenomena? However, when applying these notions of conditional property to the systematic analysis of data, we can do so in a much more direct and quantitative way. The following demonstrates the effectiveness of doing this.

It should be emphasized again that in these demonstrations, medical diagnostic testing is merely a paradigm. It is a convenient way of illustrating the value of conditional probability when we evaluate the data encountered in all fields of endeavor. In fact, it is the author's belief that the concepts of conditional probability should be considered an indispensable tool in our search for the truth about all aspects of the world in which we live.

First, the performances of diagnostic tests are imperfect. Therefore, the results of these tests should be considered in probabilistic, rather than in absolute, terms. That is why the results are typically expressed as percent sensitivity and percent specificity, rather than as unequivocal disease present versus disease absent statements. In this chapter, we have seen examples of the use of disease prevalence when applying the principles of conditional probability to the analysis of data. In many cases, though, it is hard to determine a priori what the prevalence of a condition of interest is in a particular population. Estimates of the prior probability of a disease traditionally rely on previous studies of the distributions of the disease in various demographic groups. These estimates are imprecise, partly because the epidemiological studies of the prevalence of various diseases have yielded inconsistent results. The inconsistencies are due to such factors as intrinsic differences among populations (e.g., the distributions of age and sex of the subjects), statistical sampling errors, and differences in the nature and accuracy of the tests that had been used to identify the diseases in the epidemiological studies.

In fact, attempts to stipulate the prevalence of something in a population can be somewhat circular, especially if we still have a great deal to learn about the entity that we are trying to study. If we are still in the process of developing reliable criteria for identifying a phenomenon, how can we accurately determine its true prevalence in a population?

For these reasons, I developed and tested a more precise method for using conditional probability without the need to estimate the actual prevalence of a disease in a population of data of a phenomenon of interest. The alternative to determining prevalence in a particular population is to consider the presence or absence of other entities that are known to be at least indirectly associated with the phenomena that one is trying to detect. I reasoned as follows:

- If A is a specific phenomenon that one is trying to detect, and
- B is a different, but easily detectable, condition that tends to be associated with A, then
- The prior probability that A is present is likely to be greater in a population in which B is also present than it is in a population in which B is not present.

To test this method of using conditional probability, I applied it to the detection of left ventricular systolic dysfunction (LVSD), an abnormal condition in which the heart muscle often cannot contract strongly enough to meet the metabolic needs of the patient's body. LVSD is an important medical condition because it often leads to heart failure that in turn eventuates in severe disability and premature death. In this study, the presence or absence of LVSD was definitively determined by echocardiography.

I then evaluated the diagnostic performances of two tests that are often used to diagnose LVSD and associated heart failure. One of these tests is the electronic recording of a patient's heart sounds. Specifically, these recordings can be used to detect an abnormal third heart sound (S3) by measuring the amount of low frequency acoustical energy that is present during a particular brief period of the cardiac cycle. The greater that acoustical energy, the greater is the likelihood that the patient has LVSD. Another test for LVSD and associated heart failure is brain natriuretic peptide (BNP). BNP is measured in a small sample of the patient's venous blood, and the higher the blood level of BNP that is measured, the greater is the likelihood that the patient has LVSD and heart failure. Although both the S3 and BNP are widely used tests, neither of them have 100% specificity for LVSD with heart failure, since other conditions can also be associated with increased S3 energy and/or elevated levels of BNP [1,2].

To improve the diagnostic accuracy with which the S3 and BNP can detect LVSD with heart failure, I applied the principles of conditional probability by using the ECG. The ECG is an additional diagnostic test that is frequently used to evaluate patients with known or suspected heart disease. However, because of the nature of the data that the ECG acquires, it cannot itself directly diagnose either LVSD or heart failure. In contrast, the ECG is an excellent tool for detecting the presence of prior myocardial infarction (MI), i.e., a heart attack that has afflicted a patient at some time in the past. This is highly relevant in the present context because MI often causes sufficient damage to the heart muscle that LVSD with heart failure ensues [3,4]. Therefore, LVSD is expected to be more common in patients with ECG evidence of previous MI than it is in patients without such ECG evidence. In more general terms, ECG evidence showing that a patient has had an MI at some time in the past constitutes prima facie evidence that the patient has underlying heart disease. Therefore, it is reasonable to expect that the prior probability of LVSD with heart failure is higher in individuals who have already been shown (in this case by the ECG) to have heart disease than it is in those who lack the same type of evidence of underlying heart disease.

For this reason, I tested the hypothesis that even though the ECG is not itself a test for LVSD with heart failure, it can stratify patients with respect to their prior probabilities of having this disorder. If the hypothesis is confirmed, then the ECG can be used not only to detect disorders for which ECG data are directly relevant, but also as an objective and

Table 7.2 S3 Energy for Detecting LVSD Effects of ECG Evidence of Prior MI

	All Patients ($N = 432$)	MI Absent ($N = 313$)	MI Present ($N = 119$)
Threshold*	5.66	6.00	5.19
Specificity	98%	98%	98%
Sensitivity	21%	16%	32%
Chi square**	6.2	13.5	
P value**	1×10^{-2}	2×10^{-4}	

LVSD, left ventricular systolic dysfunction; MI, myocardial infarction.
*Proprietary sound energy display value (range = 0–10 units).
**Compared to MI present.

reproducible tool for improving the detection of an even greater variety of diseases.

To test the hypothesis, I analyzed diagnostic data from 432 patients evaluated in various emergency departments for shortness of breath. The quantitative criterion for LVSD was a left ventricular ejection fraction <50% (the normal value being ≥65%). In addition, at the time of arrival in the emergency department, 432 of the patients had their heart sounds and ECGs recorded electronically, and 374 (86%) of the patients had BNP measured. ECG evidence of previous MI was considered positive if the patient had a Selvester–Wagner Q-wave score ≥1 [5]. The tests administered to the patients in the emergency department included an echocardiogram, an ECG, an electronic recording of the heart sounds, and a venous blood sample for the measurement of BNP. Based on their echocardiographic findings, the patients were divided into a group with LVSD versus a group without LVSD. Both of these groups were further divided into cohorts with versus without ECG evidence of prior MI. Table 7.2 shows the influence of ECG evidence of prior MI on the ability of the electronically recorded S3 to detect LVSD. Table 7.2 reveals that compared to the entire group of 432 patients, the sensitivity at 98% specificity of the S3 for detecting LVSD is significantly higher in the group that has ECG evidence of prior MI compared to both the entire group of patients and the cohort in which ECG evidence of MI is absent. Furthermore, the diagnostic threshold needed to reach 98% specificity is numerically lower in the cohort with ECG evidence of prior MI than it is in either the entire group or in the cohort without ECG evidence of prior MI.

Table 7.3 BNP for Detecting LVSD Effects of ECG Evidence of Prior MI			
	All Patients ($N = 374$)	MI Absent ($N = 274$)	MI Present ($N = 100$)
Threshold (pg/mL)	1740	1740	779
Specificity	98%	98%	98%
Sensitivity	11%	11%	34%
Chi square*	31.4	27.4	
P value*	2×10^{-8}	2×10^{-7}	

BNP, brain naturiuretic peptide; LVSD, left ventricular systolic dysfunction, MI, myocardial infarction.
*Compared to MI present.

Table 7.3 shows that the influence of ECG evidence of prior MI on the ability of BNP to detect LVSD is even greater than it is on the diagnostic ability of the S3. In the patients with ECG evidence of prior MI, the sensitivity of BNP at 98% specificity was approximately three times that of either the entire group of patients or of the cohort without ECG evidence of prior MI. Not surprisingly, this improvement in the diagnostic performance of BNP is highly statistically significant. In addition, the threshold of BNP needed to attain 98% diagnostic specificity is less than half of that required in either the entire group of patients or the normal cohort.

The data in Tables 7.2 and 7.3 clearly show that the presence or absence of ECG evidence of prior MI augments the abilities of the S3 and BNP to diagnose LVSD with heart failure. However, a caveat in interpreting these previous findings is that the diagnosis of MI by ECG is itself uncertain. The accuracy of the ECG diagnosis of MI depends on the skill of the electrocardiographer, on the accuracy of the diagnostic algorithms being used to make the diagnosis, and of course, on the pretest probability of MI in the patients from whom the ECGs had been recorded [6–9]. This uncertainty precludes a consistently reliable estimate of the prior probability of other types of heart disease being tested for.

This raises the possibility that using other types of ECG data would be even more desirable. Just as the S3 and BNP have imperfect sensitivity and specificity for detecting LVSD with heart failure, the ECG often makes errors in the detection of prior MI [6–9]. Consequently, ECG evidence of prior MI would incorrectly identify some patients as having or not having underlying heart disease. To address this problem, I tried providing

Table 7.4 S3 Sound Energy for Detecting LVSD Effects of Prolonged ECG–QRS Complex

	All Patients ($N = 432$)	QRS >120 ($N = 107$)	QRS >140 ($N = 65$)
Threshold*	5.66	4.99	4.99
Specificity	98%	98%	98%
Sensitivity	21%	32%	43%
Chi square**		3.84	11.2
P value**		5.0×10^{-2}	8.2×10^{-4}

LVSD, left ventricular systolic dysfunction; QRS, QRS complex duration in milliseconds.
*Proprietary measurement of heart sound energy.
**Compared to all patients.

background information about the patients using a more precise and reproducible type of ECG abnormality than evidence of prior MI.

The parameter that I chose for this part of the evaluation is the duration of the ECG–QRS complex. The duration of the QRS complex is expressed in milliseconds (ms) and represents the total time required for electrical activation (depolarization) of the ventricles. Since most ECG machines are digital instruments that use both high sampling rates and precise computerized measurements, QRS complex duration is determined with great accuracy, and its numerical value is included in each ECG diagnostic report. Therefore, the ECG–QRS duration is a precise, highly reproducible and readily available parameter for assessing the prior probability of underlying heart disease in each member of a population of patients. The upper limit of normal for ECG–QRS complex duration is 100 ms. Values of ECG–QRS duration between 100 ms and 120 ms are often considered borderline.

To evaluate the ability of the ECG–QRS duration to augment the abilities of the S3 and BNP to diagnose heart failure, I studied the same 432 patients that had been used in the investigation of the use of ECG evidence of previous MI. In the present study, I divided the entire group of patients into two cohorts of QRS >120 ms and QRS >140 ms, respectively. Obviously, the QRS >140 ms group is a subclass of the QRS >120 ms group.

Tables 7.4 and 7.5 show the effects of prolonged ECG–QRS duration on the respective abilities of the S3 and BNP to diagnose LVSD with heart failure. Table 7.4 shows that in the cohort of patients with

Table 7.5 BNP for Detecting LVSD Effects of Prolonged ECG–QRS Complex			
	All Patients (N = 374)	QRS >120 (N = 93)	QRS >140 (N = 58)
Threshold (pg/mL)	1740	407	148
Specificity	98%	98%	98%
Sensitivity	11%	47%	82%
Chi square*		41.2	101
P value*		1.4×10^{-10}	9.2×10^{-24}

LVSD, left ventricular systolic dysfunction; QRS, QRS complex duration in milliseconds.
*Compared to all patients.

ECG–QRS complex duration >120 ms, the S3 has a statistically significantly higher sensitivity for LVSD than does the entire group of patients. In the cohort with ECG–QRS duration >140 ms, there is a further increase in sensitivity at 98% specificity.

Table 7.5 shows that the presence of prolonged ECG–QRS duration has an even more marked effect on the performance of BNP for detecting LVSD with heart failure. ECG–QRS duration >120 ms is associated with a very highly significant increase in the diagnostic sensitivity of BNP compared to the entire group. In the cohort with ECG–QRS >140 ms, there is a further marked increase in the sensitivity of BNP for LVSD.

The observation that prolonged QRS duration augments the diagnostic performances for detecting LVSD of both S3 acoustical energy and BNP raises the question of whether QRS duration by itself is a useful parameter for detecting LVSD. However, analysis of the QRS data revealed that the diagnostic sensitivity at 98% specificity for LVSD of the parameter QRS duration is only 20% (at a corresponding threshold value of 151 ms).

Comparing this performance to the data in Table 7.4 shows that the diagnostic performance of the QRS duration by itself is statistically significantly inferior to the performances of S3 acoustical energy in patients with QRS durations of 120 ms and 140 ms, respectively – chi square = 3.84 ($p = 5 \times 10^{-2}$) and chi square = 11.20 ($p = 8 \times 10^{-4}$). Comparing the diagnostic performance of the QRS duration by itself to the data in Table 7.5 shows that it is also statistically significantly inferior to the performances of BNP in patients with QRS durations of 120 ms and 140 ms, respectively – chi square = 20.3 ($p = 6.6 \times 10^{-6}$) and chi square = 69.9 ($p = 6.2 \times 10^{-17}$). Therefore, as a parameter for diagnosing LVSD, using QRS duration alone is inferior to combining prolonged QRS duration with either S3 acoustical energy or BNP. In keeping with the principles of conditional probability, prolonged QRS duration can be considered to be a "background" condition in which to interpret the S3 and the BNP data. For example, the results shown last column of Table 7.5 could be read, "Conditional upon the presence of a QRS duration greater than 140 ms, a BNP value >148 pg/mL has 82% sensitivity and 98% specificity for detecting LVSD."

Considering the nature of population of patients in which they were tested, the magnitudes of the effects of the ECG findings of prior MI and of prolonged QRS duration are especially remarkable. All the patients used in each study had presented to emergency departments with shortness of breath. Therefore, the population studied already had a much higher prevalence of LVSD with heart failure than does the general population. The fact that the ECG findings of prior MI and prolonged QRS duration had such strong incremental effects on the detection of LVSD with heart failure suggests that these ECG abnormalities are especially powerful determinants of prior probability.

This chapter has provided both an explanation of the principles of conditional probability and has shown evidence to support their use in the analysis of data. However, many readers may wish to have more information about the subject and may encounter discussions of probability elsewhere. For these readers, there now follows a description of the symbolic notation often used in working with the principles of conditional probability. This includes the symbols that are used to express the ideas conveyed in the famous and important Bayes' theorem [10].

BAYES' THEOREM AND THE SYMBOLS USED IN CONDITIONAL PROBABILITY

Table 7.6 shows a system of notation that is often used to express statements about probability:

Regarding general principles of conditional probability that were discussed earlier in the chapter:

Table 7.6 Symbolic Notations Used in Probability Statements

Probability Expression	Meaning of the Expression
h	Hypothesis to be tested
e	Evidence supporting the hypothesis
b	Background information used to help evaluate the evidence
P	Probability
|	An operator that means "given that," "if," or "conditional upon"
~	An operator that means "not"
$P(h)$	Probability that the hypothesis is correct
$P(h \mid e)$	Probability that the hypothesis is correct, given the evidence
$P(h \mid b)$	Probability that the hypothesis is correct, given the background information
$P(h \mid e,b)$	Probability that the hypothesis is correct, given both the evidence and the background information
$P(e \mid h,b)$	Probability that the evidence is present, given the background Information and the fact that the hypothesis is correct
$P(\sim h)$	Probability that the hypothesis is not correct
$P(\sim h \mid e)$	Probability that the hypothesis is not correct, given the evidence
$P(\sim h \mid b)$	Probability that the hypothesis is not correct, given the background information
$P(\sim h \mid e,b)$	Probability that the hypothesis is not correct, given the evidence and the background information
$P(e \mid \sim h,b)$	Probability that the evidence is present, given the background information and the fact that the hypothesis is not correct

- $P(h \mid b)$ = the prior (or pre-test) probability, i.e., the probability that the hypothesis is correct conditional upon the available background information
- $P(h \mid e,b)$ = posterior (or post-test) probability, i.e., the probability that the hypothesis is correct, conditional upon both the available evidence and background information

Using the paradigm of diagnostic testing:

- $P(e \mid h)$ = diagnostic sensitivity based on the test results alone. For a particular test for a disease, it expresses the probability of having a positive result on that test every time the disease is present. This is also called the non-Bayesian diagnostic sensitivity, since it does not consider the effects of any background conditions.
- $P(e \mid h,b)$ = diagnostic sensitivity based on both the test results and the background information. It also expresses the probability of

having a positive result on a test every time the disease is present, conditional upon the relevant background conditions being present. It is also called the Bayesian diagnostic sensitivity because it does consider at least one relevant background condition.

- $P(h \mid e)$ = diagnostic specificity based on the test results alone. For each positive result of a test for a particular disease, it expresses the probability that the test's positive result is associated with the actual presence of that particular disease. This is also called the non-Bayesian diagnostic specificity, since it does not consider the effects of any background conditions in addition to the result of the test.
- $P(h \mid e,b)$ = diagnostic specificity based on both the test results and the background information. For each positive result on the test that occurs in the context of relevant background information, it expresses the probability that the positive test result is associated with the actual presence of the disease being tested for. It is also called the Bayesian diagnostic specificity, since it does consider at least one relevant background condition.

BAYESIAN STATISTICS AND BAYES' THEOREM

Bayesian statistics is a set of procedures for solving problems that involve conditional probability. It is named after the Reverend Thomas Bayes, a clergyman and mathematician who lived in England from 1701 to 1761.

The following is an expression of Bayes theorem that looks somewhat daunting, but it merely uses the symbols that were defined in Table 7.6. It is important to remember that since the expression is an actual theorem, it means that it has been formally proven to be mathematically valid. A purpose of showing this formal expression of the theorem is to reinforce some of the underlying concepts of conditional probability.

EXPRESSION OF BAYES' THEOREM IN SYMBOLS

$$P(h \mid e,b) = \frac{P(h \mid b) \times P(e \mid h,b)}{[P(h \mid b) \times P(e \mid h,b)] + [P(\sim h \mid b) \times P(e \mid \sim h,b)]}$$

The above equation states that the probability of a hypothesis given both the direct evidence for the hypothesis and the relevant background information equals:

the probability of the hypothesis given only the background information

times

the probability of this evidence being present given both the truth of the hypothesis and the background information

divided by

the numerator of the expression plus the negation of the numerator

The negation of the numerator is the probability that the hypothesis is not true given the same evidence and background information in the numerator. Since the denominator of the expression contains the sum of the numerator and its negation, it accounts for all the possibilities regarding the hypothesis, i.e., that it is either true or false. Therefore, expressed as a percentage, the denominator always equals 100%. If, for example, the value of $P(h \mid b) \times P(e \mid h,b)$ is 60%, the value of the expression is 60%/100% or 60% – the same value as that of the numerator.

A detailed discussion of the numerous applications of Bayes' theorem is well beyond the scope of this book. However, this theorem demonstrates that the use of conditional probability that is being advocated in this chapter has a sound mathematical basis. Second, the evidence that has been presented in the chapter to demonstrate the importance of using background information when testing hypotheses has shown that using conditional probability also has a sound scientific basis as well.

REFERENCES

[1] Marcus GM, Gerber L, McKeown BH. Association between phonocardiographic third and fourth heart sounds and objective measures of left ventricular function. JAMA 2005;293: 2238–44.

[2] Waku S, Iida N, Ishihara T. Significance of brain natriuretic peptide measurement as a diagnostic indicator of cardiac function. Method Inform Med 2000;39:249–53.

[3] Gheorghiade M, Bonow RO. Chronic heart failure in the United States: a manifestation of coronary artery disease. Circulation 1998;97:282–9.

[4] He J, Ogden LG, Bazzano LA, Vupputuri S. Risk factors for congestive heart failure in US men and women: NHANES I epidemiologic follow-up study. Arch Intern Med 2001;161(7): 996–1002.

[5] Selvester RH, Wagner GS, Hindman NB. The Selvester QRS scoring system for estimating myocardial infarct size the development and application of the system. Arch Intern Med 1985;145(10):1877–81.

[6] Warner RA. Improving medical diagnosis by using digital data to assess the prior probability of disease. Proceedings of the 2013 International Conference on Bioinformatics and Computational Biology. 2013. pp. 62–65.

[7] Warner RA, Hill NE. Optimized electrocardiographic criteria for prior inferior and an anterior myocardial infarction. J Electrocardiol 2012;45:209–13.

[8] Wagner GS, Maynard C, Andresen A, Anderson E, Myers R, Warner RA, Selvester RH. The evaluation of advanced electrocardiographic diagnostic software for detection of prior myocardial infarction. Am J Cardiol 2002;89(Suppl 10):75–9.

[9] Elko P, Warner RA. Using directly-acquired digital EKG data to optimize the diagnostic criteria for anterior myocardial infarction. J Electrocardiol 1994;(Supplemental Issue):S89–92.

[10] Efron B. Bayes' theorem in the 21st century. Science 2013;340:1177–8.